Amanda Slavin is one of those special people that you wish you could clone to make the world a better place, but at the same time, you're a little scared to clone her because so much information comes out of her at 100 miles per hour that there's no way you can keep up with more than one Amanda. So I was excited to hear that she was able to capture everything that was in her head and coming out of her mouth into something printed on paper.

One of the philosophies I try to live by (and use for employee all-hands meetings) is ICEE (an acronym I made up to help with remembering): Inspire, Connect, Educate, and Entertain. Amanda's Seventh Level of Engagement framework resonates with the way I think about business and life, so it's not surprising that Amanda and I get along so well since her self-described Seventh Level (which I found out about after I read this book) is about "building connections while inspiring and educating others."

I'd recommend this book for anyone looking to change their organization for the better by connecting more meaningfully to employees, customers, or other stakeholders. And the good news is it's much easier to get additional copies of this book than it is to clone additional copies of Amanda.

—TONY HSIEH, AUTHOR OF #1 *NEW YORK TIMES* BESTSELLER *DELIVERING HAPPINESS*, AND CEO OF ZAPPOS.COM

THE SEVENTH LEVEL

THE
SEVENTH
LEVEL

Transform Your Business
Through Meaningful Engagement with
Your Customers and Employees

AMANDA SLAVIN

LIONCREST
PUBLISHING

THE SEVENTH LEVEL

Transform Your Business Through Meaningful
Engagement with Your Customers and Employees

ISBN   978-1-5445-0581-7 *Hardcover*
        978-1-5445-0580-0 *Paperback*
        978-1-5445-0579-4 *Ebook*

CONTENTS

INTRODUCTION

The age of passive consumerism is dead. Welcome to the age of active participants, of creators, of people that want to be heard, seen, and rewarded for having a perspective. Over the past twenty years, the culture has shifted to where people no longer passively consume but actively participate in connecting with your brand. Your customers now have tools at their fingertips which allow them to amplify their criticisms, feelings, and thoughts about your company. Customers have always had the chance to give feedback, but now these customers have their own audiences, their own followings, and this directly affects you! Customers are no longer just the purchasers of your product, but people that can serve as an extension of your sales team. They "sell" for you when they advocate for you, follow you, connect with you, and are interested in what you have to say as a brand. Just think about what is more impactful: When you tell everyone how great you are? Or when your most loyal brand advocates rave about how wonderful you are to their friends, family, and followers? There are countless ways to connect with these customers, and it is no longer as simple and straightforward as being one of the only brands to sell a product. Companies that have been around for hundreds of years can disappear in an instant if an upstart competitor co-opts their market share by earning more brand loyalty through deeper customer connections.

One of the most common—and historically effective— ways to communicate directly with large swaths of a customer base is through marketing. But even that is changing. Today, the average customer sees five thousand ads a day.[1] People are tired of it! Customers' attention is spread thinner than ever, and attention is a precious resource. So as companies, it is imperative that we change the way we are thinking about our relationship to both our internal and external customers. Whether it's an employee—an internal customer—leaving a review on Glassdoor, your most devoted fan making their usual purchase and then telling their friends and family about it, or a customer boasting about you on Instagram, as a brand, you have a responsibility to engage with your customers in a way that's respectful of their time and limited

---

1   John Simpson, "Finding Brand Success in the Digital World," *Forbes*, August 25, 2017, https://www.forbes.com/sites/forbesagencycouncil/2017/08/25/ finding-brand-success-in-the-digital-world/#172fc919626e.

attention. How can we engage and meaningfully connect with our customers when there are so many tools at our disposal, and so many definitions of what engagement even means?

We want our employees and customers to be our brand advocates, carrying our flag proudly and waving it in the air; we want them to care because we've inspired them, not because we told them they should.

A lonely teenager feels like an outcast at her high school, but one day hears a Lady Gaga song on the radio that resonates with her. The self-affirming lyrics click with this student and give her hope and confidence. She becomes a "Little Monster"—a Gaga superfan—and never misses a concert when her hero comes to her state. She joins a message board for fans and discovers a sense of community. Her identity becomes intertwined with Lady Gaga's brand, which helps her through her difficult teenage years.

A recent college graduate leaves a job fair on campus in disappointment. None of the recruiters seem to get it— they only talk about money and company status. This young woman wants to make a living, sure. But she also wants to lead a balanced, purposeful life that features lots of hiking, yoga, and surfing. So she applies for and lands a job at Patagonia—a company whose values align perfectly with her own. As her friends bounce from job to job throughout their early twenties, she's the anomaly. She stays at Patagonia, loves every second of it, and encourages her like-minded friends to apply for any and all openings at her company.

A fifty-two-year-old man who is tired of punching the clock at work every day saves up enough money to buy a used motorcycle—a Harley-Davidson. He plans a short road trip, which turns into a cross-country adventure, before having to go back to work. He feels free and liberated and associates that feeling with his Harley. After another decade of hard work and setting aside a portion of his paycheck each week, he buys a brand-new motorcycle: a Harley-Davidson—it had to be a Harley.

Think about the experiences in your life that have shaped you, that have made you, *you*, that have spoken to you, that have connected to you in a way that is beyond visceral. The sum of those feelings is the Seventh Level. We all go through life striving for meaningful connections. But that doesn't always have to mean connection with a person. Sometimes the most meaningful connections in our lives are with a job, or experience, or piece of art, or brand.

Apple has played a huge role in shaping my identity. As an entrepreneur, it helped me launch my career. My old MacBook was the first laptop that I bought for myself, that

I wasn't forced to use by an employer. It was beautiful and sleek and special and felt more like a gorgeous piece of jewelry than a computer. It made me feel in charge and creative, and now I refuse to buy anything except Apple.

Maybe it was those old "Mac vs PC" commercials with Justin Long, or reading Steve Jobs's autobiography that contributed to my Apple-only policy. But what ultimately matters most is what I have made Apple mean for *me*— how my personal values and beliefs of inspiring and educating aligned with what I would say is Steve Jobs's Seventh Level Statement: to create beautiful things that inspire the way people see themselves and the world.

The Seventh Level of Engagement is pervasive throughout culture, time, and context. It's when your personal values and beliefs align with another's message, when you derive meaning and even identity from connecting with this brand, person, or concept.

It's when you camp out overnight to be first in line for concert tickets. It's when you forego the conventional career route in favor of one that allows you to sell something you're proud of—and also surf during your lunch break. It's when you ride your motorcycle to the tattoo parlor, then ask the artist to tattoo an image of that same motorcycle onto your arm. And it's when I drop my phone for the umpteenth time, it finally breaks, then I drop whatever I was doing to hustle to the Apple store to get a replacement because I don't feel like myself without my iPhone.

The Seventh Level of Engagement, which is defined as Literate Thinking, signifies alignment and resonance with a brand and the values and beliefs that brand embraces. Advocates, ambassadors, and loyalists feel that the brand and what it stands for embody who they are. At the Seventh Level, customers are active participants in building and supporting the brands, companies, people, employers, or ideas they love.

DEFINING ENGAGEMENT

Before we go any further, we need to establish one thing. What do I mean by engagement?

I define engagement as authentic, meaningful human connection that leads to the granting of time and attention.

It's important to remember that when I talk about engagement and its definition, I am talking about humans, not just metrics. Most of the engagement examples I will discuss in this book pertain to business. But engagement as defined above absolutely applies to every aspect of your interpersonal life as well.

Engagement impacts where real people choose to allocate their time, their energy, their attention. What a person decides to engage in is important and should not be taken lightly—as I discussed earlier, attention is a finite resource and should be treated as such!

The reason this might be confusing is that "engagement" has become this amorphous buzzword that people overuse without really understanding what it means or how much power it has. In more common parlance, we talk about engagement to describe how many or how much of a desired action is taken. It's the term *du jour* not only for marketing directors, social media mavens, and content gurus, but also for CEOs, HR executives, directors, "influencers," teachers, speakers, marriage counselors... well, really anyone who deals with human beings on a regular basis!

It's no surprise, really. We live in a data-driven world. We measure employee effectiveness by measures of productivity—and productivity is directly correlated to an employee's degree of engagement. We measure the effectiveness of our online content by how engaging it is, so it's only natural for people to use the word a lot—and I mean a lot. The word engagement gets thrown around as the problem and the solution without anyone taking a step back and evaluating what engagement is and how to make it happen.

We know engagement is important but often don't know how to define it. We tend to think of engagement as binary: a person is either engaged or disengaged, but it's really much, much more nuanced than that. Engagement is not a frothy, fluffy word, or a binary concept. There are seven distinct levels, and engagement has a direct impact on your bottom line.

Consider this: a Gallup survey reports that fully engaged customers account for a 23 percent share of profitability.[2] On the employee side, 71 percent of people rank employee engagement as essential to a thriving workplace. The conundrum appears when I read—in another Gallup survey—that 87 percent of US employees are disengaged, which costs the US $450–500 billion a year in productivity. This means engagement is important to two-thirds of the population, but less than 15 percent are engaged! We've never been given a universal definition and road map when it comes to engagement, so of course we are just trying different things to see what sticks, without any real structure. You wouldn't go on a vacation you didn't do any planning for, right? If you traveled this spontaneously, you'd be resigned to paying a whole lot more for last-minute flights and accommodations. Why would you begin your journey to greater customer engagement without an itinerary or road map?

---

2   "Turning Customers into True Believers: Customer Engagement," Gallup, https://www.gallup.com/services/169331/customer-engagement.aspx.

We can agree that engagement is a key factor in profitability, but where do we even begin? Marketing Insider Group found that customers don't interact as much as they would because companies send too much content that doesn't matter to them.[3] Think about the feeling you have when you receive content that has nothing to do with you. I recently asked an audience at a conference to tell me how they felt when this happened, and they all responded with a collective *ugh*. Customers want to be seen, heard, and know they matter, and they also want to know if they are giving you their time and energy, that you are also doing the same to respond, as if you were talking to them one-on-one (even if it is one-on-one million). With all of the tools at our disposal, it is our responsibility to determine the most suitable steps to connect with our customers and recognize it is a two-way street, like any relationship. It is no longer as easy as shoving our product down their throats because of how many choices they have to allocate their money and their time.

Over the past ten years, I've seen the definition of engagement change too many times to count—whether it pertains to employee engagement, marketing engagement, or engagement in our personal lives. I've witnessed the overwhelming number of tools introduced and

3   Michael Brenner, "The Top Marketing Challenges in the Engagement Economy," *Marketing Insider Group*, September 5, 2017, https://marketinginsidergroup.com/content-marketing/marketing-challenges-engagement-economy/.

brought to market with the goal of measuring or increasing engagement—from employee productivity tools to social media platforms to an increase in experiential marketing budgets to inbound marketing campaigns. We have all these tools at our fingertips (literally on our phones), but we constantly make the same mistakes because no one taught us how to properly use them, or they aren't equipped to measure the depth of engagement—just quantity.

At its core, engagement is capturing the attention of each other in all aspects of our lives—business and personal. Engagement is the invisible force that guides our experiences and our decision-making. It is the bedrock of human connection.

Whether in business or in our personal lives, we all want meaningful connections. With relationships, we want closeness and understanding, and in business, we want to not only survive but thrive. We want brand loyalists and advocates who will show us that we are not alone and who will help us grow.

While there are plenty of tools to measure employee engagement—and there have been for years—the meaning of engagement has been muddled even more since social media commandeered the term. Social media tools are now telling us what engagement success is, and the tools that we should be using to meet our goals are actually setting our goals. Since social media disrupted the marketing space, we are now settling for what we have been told is engagement, which are likes, comments, and follows when we could be using technology to engage in more meaningful ways. Unfortunately, we are settling for vanity metrics that only represent lower levels of engagement without realizing there is more to the picture. Short, quick connections aren't enough; we're craving emotion and people caring about people. We spend so much time and effort communicating with our internal and external customers, what would the world look like if we connected with them with greater intention?

Understanding and harnessing engagement allows you to build connections with human beings that drive belief and action—whether you are in marketing, sales, or human resources. The problem is that we don't know where to begin. We have a plethora of communication tools to share our message, our brand, and ourselves, but we don't know how to communicate real intention behind our thoughts, nor do we have a valid way of measuring whether those messages are effective in connecting with our customers.

Marketers are obsessed with numbers and data, but are we even looking at the right numbers? In the past, even I have found myself in a role in which I've helped brands accumulate Instagram followers, only to ask myself the questions, "Why are we doing this?" or "What is the real intention here?" When most people say they want higher engagement, they mean that they want to see more "likes" or "comments" on the content they've posted to Facebook or Instagram or LinkedIn. This is proof that we've fallen into the trap of letting our social media tools dictate what we should want, instead of utilizing them to meet our own goals. Who said abundant likes and comments were more significant than what the comments actually say? We are measuring quantity over quality. Technically, we're measuring specific, limited actions, but we're not measuring whether those actions are evidence of a meaningful connection with our message. When gathered in the traditional, social-media platform-driven way, these types of measurements result in empty, useless data. The problem is, we're not evaluating how those tools can better serve us. We are not measuring personal connection—again, the thing we all crave. Instead, we've been stuck in a popularity contest of our own making. We need to take back control. We can't keep letting the tools we use tell us how to define engagement. We need to redefine engagement to align with the meaningful human connection we want.

Online engagement is one way that can help us make informed decisions about our business. The data provided to us is not the end-all, be-all of engagement; it is one aspect of engagement. Even so, we so often forget that those numbers (likes, followers, shares) represent actual human beings! We need a new way to think about engagement that will withstand the test of time. The tools of engagement are rapidly changing, and so we need to ensure we aren't letting these tools define our engagement success.

Thus, it's important that we have intention when we assess data and use technology to target solutions. We need to focus on the human beings behind the numbers, with personal values and beliefs that drive their decision-making. Authentic human engagement is the objective, which means measuring more meaningful connections than the metrics social media tools give us. How do we define and identify what meaningful engagement looks like for brands with all their people—inside their companies and with their customers? How do we holistically review and assess engagement and help humans connect with each other better, and why does this even matter?

What we need is a common language and framework to understand how we can meaningfully engage and connect with one another. That's why I developed the Seventh Level Engagement Framework. This is a structure for creating engagement, for garnering the attention of your employees and customers. It is also a road map for creative solutions to directly impact your business—the business of connecting with others.

Seventh Level Engagement happens when your personal values and beliefs align with a message; when you feel deeply connected to someone, something, or some brand; and when it becomes a part of you. The Seventh Level Engagement Framework has seven distinct levels of engagement that can help you identify a path to a meaningful transaction between two human beings.

Whether you're a marketing director working for a Fortune 500 company, a CEO of a small business, or a sole proprietor, the Seventh Level of Engagement Framework can work for you. Businesses are made of people, so engagement impacts every aspect of the business from the employer to employee, from the company to their customers. And that's not even looking at the world at large, outside of business! I have spent my entire career analyzing how people engage, both professionally and personally, and have seen this framework bring success to a multitude of businesses and people.

It can work for you too.

THE SEVENTH LEVEL ENGAGEMENT FRAMEWORK

Ten years ago, when I was working on my thesis paper

for my masters in curriculum and instruction, I began to research engagement and came across an engagement taxonomy, or categorization system, created by two education professors, Robert Bangert-Drowns and Curtis Pyke. They analyzed the behavior of students interacting with a software program and identified seven levels of engaged behavior. I was inspired by their taxonomy and sought to apply it to a qualitative measurement system, which had never been done before.

To this end, my colleagues and I analyzed thirty students in two different environments: indoors (using technology as the teaching tool) and outdoors (using nature as the teaching tool). We measured students' engagement and actions through surveys, interviews, and time sampling. We determined that higher levels of engagement led to higher levels of achievement.

Achievement is critical in everything we do, not only in learning but also in life. Regardless of where we are in life's journey, we are focused on goals: getting an A, landing a sale, connecting in our relationships, and so on. What we don't often realize is that it takes engagement to achieve our goals.

Based on the results of my analysis, I adapted the renowned work of Bangert-Drowns and Pyke into the Seventh Level Engagement Framework to empower people with a language to define, understand, and improve engagement with their audience, whether that be employees or customers.

We're faced with more distractions and demands than ever before, resulting in ever-dwindling time and attention to dedicate to creating meaningful connections. The Framework provides a step-by-step approach to put all our efforts to creating connections in one place. It offers clarity through the hazy way we currently attempt to connect. This framework will change the way you think about yourself and your relationships with your customers, your colleagues, your employees, your boss—it may even permeate your relationships with your family, friends, and significant others.

I think of all these people as your "audience," a term I apply to anyone with whom you want to build engagement, whether that be a group of students, employees within a company, a customer, your social media followers, a sales lead, or event attendees about to hear your keynote speech. Your audience, in the context of this book, represents a group of people or a single person on the receiving end of your message. And the Seventh Level Engagement Framework exists to help you more deeply, purposefully, and effectively engage with your audience.

As I have mentioned, the Seventh Level Engagement

Framework is comprised of seven distinct levels of engagement. These seven levels fall into three phases (based on the inbound tool, HubSpot's marketing flywheel, which you can learn more about in the appendix). Before you can start utilizing the Seventh Level Engagement Framework, you need to first take a look inward and draft your Seventh Level Statement.

In the following chapters, I will first walk you through creating your Seventh Level Statement and then break down Levels One through Six, leading to the Seventh Level. In these sections, I'll explain their significance and offer examples of how to work through the framework.

PHASE 1: ATTRACT

The attract stage comprises the levels that are about earning audience trust:

- Level One: Disengagement. *Who is your audience?*
- Level Two: Unsystematic Engagement. *Do they understand your message?*
- Level Three: Frustrated Engagement. *What distracts your audience?*

PHASE 2: ENGAGE

Now that you have earned your audience's trust, you

can start to ask something of them. The following levels within the engage stage help you to interact further with your audience and build a deeper bond.

- Level Four: Structure-Dependent Engagement. *What are you asking them to do?*
- Level Five: Self-Regulated Interest. *What excites your audience?*

PHASE 3: DELIGHT

This stage is focused on delighting, inspiring, and empowering your audience. These levels of engagement occur when your message meaningfully aligns with your audience's personal values and beliefs, allowing you to transition them from customers to brand loyalists.

- Level Six: Critical Engagement. *How do you inspire them to set goals?*
- Seventh Level: Literate Thinking. *How do your audience's personal values and beliefs deeply align with yours?*

WHY DO YOU NEED THIS BOOK?

Executives, directors, and thought leaders actively work to transform their corporate culture, both internally and externally. This book is for you whether you're an executive looking to change your organization for the better or are frustrated with the current tools available as well as the current limiting definitions of engagement that keep us disconnected, disengaged, and misinformed. This book is for you if you're trying to understand the process by which people hear, understand, and then connect with a message.

We are settling for a one-way conversation when we could be building more meaningful and more profitable connections. The Seventh Level Engagement Framework can help you create a meaningful connection with other humans—be they employees, customers, peers, or stakeholders—and make changes within your company to increase engagement.

Since work is comprised of human beings and sales are meaningful transactions between two human beings, this book may end up also helping you with your relationships across the board. When you are striving for meaningful connection, taking ownership of your own efforts, and working toward connecting with someone from your and their personal values and beliefs, your relationships start to shift. This framework will help you assess and identify where and how your personal relationships are connecting with you and how to deepen the relationship.

I lay out the framework for understanding how internal and external customer interactions with an organization build emotional connections that are essential to surviving in the modern market. You will learn how to connect with today's customers, both inside and outside of your organization. Yes, these days, your employees are your most important customers of all.

You will learn how to create meaningful relationships with everyone around you, online or otherwise. Within these pages, I will teach you how this method can be used in the workplace, customer acquisition, and personal relationships to elevate your engagement game.

APATHY IS THE ENEMY

We live in a time where infinite information is at our fingertips. Although it offers huge advantages and is generally looked upon as a good thing, it also has some significant drawbacks. The vast amount of available information leads to information overload. We are inundated with so much of it that it's hard to process it all. This inability to process has created a generation of people who are overwhelmed and jaded, which then leads to apathy.

People often think disengagement is the opposite of engagement, but it is not. Apathy is. Disengagement is actually the first level of engagement in the Seventh Level Engagement Framework.

The more apathetic we become, the more we find ourselves constantly sharing what we feel without thinking about how it impacts others or listening to them. Apathy, also known as indifference, leads to not considering the perspectives and feelings of others. This framework is about looking at yourself and bettering yourself versus blaming your audience—be that an employee, customer, your boss, or partner—which creates apathetic workplaces and disgruntled customers.

After speaking onstage with brilliant marketers Daniel Pink and Cal Fussman as part of a Chicago Ideas Week presentation on millennial consumer behavior, I had the chance to meet with a group of Generation Z kids— eighteen-year-olds from the Chicago public school system—and I asked them if they liked it when advertisers followed them with irrelevant products on social media. The answer was a resounding *no*. They hate advertisers.

We've created an entire generation that despises the way things are marketed to them. They see right through our stalking efforts. And yet, marketing is the primary pathway available to us to elicit behavior change. Imagine when we're trying to market to the younger generations about decisions that can impact our planet. There has to be a break in inundating people and hijacking their lives with content they don't want to see.

ENGAGEMENT IS THE ANTIDOTE TO APATHY

A more engaged world is a more inspired world where people connect with each other and with things that they care about—and to me that's what everyone's striving for. Engagement, then, is the antidote to apathy. Yet our limited descriptions and definitions of engagement keep us confined to the way that we think about relationships, work, and sales, making everything transactional.

We as human beings have always craved community and connection. We are seeking out places that make us feel human. We mimic behavior that our ancestors created. It started with talks around a fire when humans worked side by side as hunters and gatherers, and the campfire chats are now Reddit conversations, and the hunting and gathering groups are now in coworking and collaborative spaces all around the world.

Engagement leads to curiosity and a desire to learn from those who have different opinions. The Seventh Level Engagement Framework is one of learning and teaching, not one of talking *at* people. Rather than blaming others for what they have done wrong or how they have communicated poorly or why they don't understand your thoughts, this framework puts the ownership on the person who is trying to connect with someone else. It guides the individual to look at their own behaviors and what they can do better instead of pointing the finger at others.

Whether you are launching a new business, product, website, or creative campaign, looking for sponsors for an event, or trying out a new work structure with your employees, you are communicating a new message. Without a road map, any project that communicates a new message lacks structure or guidance. This is where the framework comes in.

We are constantly working to connect with people but don't really know where to begin. We reinvent the wheel every time or depend on outside marketers to tell us exactly what to do rather than equipping ourselves to do it. As you think about how to use this framework, think about the driving reason why you would want to connect with your audience more deeply. Is it to increase sales? Do you need to increase employee engagement? Do you want to market a new idea? Are you launching a new product? Building a business from the ground up? Trying to get people to attend an event or experience? Trying to recruit members or donors? What is your overall strategy where you can use this framework to determine success?

While this framework can be used by your marketing team to create an overarching engagement strategy, it can also be used for a specific project, and across your entire organization. Your sales team, your HR team, your marketing team, your engineering team, and your design team will all speak the same language, which means *finally* we are all speaking the same language when it comes to engagement. We shift from living in silos with our own metrics of success to being on the same page moving toward the same goals as a team.

ENGAGING TO INSPIRE AND EDUCATE

As a sophomore in college, I entered a rigorous five-year bachelor's/master's program for education. While working toward this degree, I needed money on the side, so I planned events in New York City on weekends and holidays. When I began student teaching, I realized that while I loved teaching, I also looked forward to the highly variable and dynamic atmosphere I found working in the world of events.

By the time I graduated in 2009, during the biggest recession I have ever lived through, budgets were being slashed and teachers were not very sought after—it was a mess! Instead of entering the teaching field, I continued working in the hospitality industry as a marketing and events director, as there was a job available immediately.

While, at the time, I was disappointed that I wouldn't be putting my teaching degree directly to use, I quickly learned that education and nightlife/hospitality are more similar than I could have ever imagined. Believe me: getting the attention of first graders feels a whole lot like trying to garner the attention of a bunch of drunk bankers! As a teacher, I nurtured a community of students. Now I was developing a community of customers. And if I could sell math to a six-year-old, I knew I could sell anything to anyone. In both spaces, success was rooted in establishing meaningful connections, and I started to see how deeply emotions are tied in to connection.

All along the way, from teaching to marketing, I used the concept I wrote my thesis on, the Seventh Level Engagement Framework, as my secret sauce. When I was a first-grade student-teacher, each morning, I asked members of my class to sit in a circle and talk about anything they wanted to for one minute—I wanted to get to know them. I did the same thing with my customers when I worked in hospitality. I emailed each and every customer and asked them how their experience was, personally responding to their needs. I started to understand their personal values and beliefs and was able to build a community based on what mattered most to them.

As I dove deeper into marketing, I discovered that the same emphasis on connection, attention, and engagement I employed in teaching could pay off in my new field. If you actually know a person, and then make that person feel seen and understood, they'll be way more loyal than if you try to sell them an open bar package without any acknowledgment of their needs.

I believe that as marketers we have a responsibility, since we have some of the biggest "classrooms" (audiences) in the world. We are changing people's behavior, culture, and impacting their perspectives of themselves and the world. Good, intentional marketing educates and inspires people to change behavior for the better.

The Seventh Level Engagement Framework can provide a road map for intentional engagement that educates and inspires—whether in marketing, sales, education, or even just having a conversation. I used the Framework to better understand how to teach my students how to tell time but also how to build an award-winning, multimillion-dollar brand in the hospitality industry. The same sort of focus, thought, and consideration went into both efforts! So, when I started my company CatalystCreativ in 2012, it was a no-brainer to continue applying the Framework. It's enhanced my understanding of engagement as it pertains to Fortune 100 companies, startups, nonprofits, and even individuals seeking to meaningfully connect with their customers.

And now, after having utilized the Seventh Level Engagement Framework since 2009 as my secret sauce in the work I have done in education, hospitality, branding, marketing, and events, the educator in me felt it was time to teach the world about this new method of thinking about engagement.

My dream is for the world to be a more engaged, inspired place, full of people who are passionate about the work they do, intentional about the things they buy and the way they connect with each other, and that emphasizes understanding human engagement.

In order to develop engagement with others, however, we have to begin with ourselves. We are at a point in time where connection is the most significant factor in changing our personal trajectories away from a path of apathy.

Shall we begin?

PART ONE

ACTIVATE FROM WITHIN

Chapter One

START WITH YOUR SEVENTH LEVEL STATEMENT

The Seventh Level is the pinnacle of engagement, and it's the goal that the Seventh Level Engagement Framework propels you toward. To be clear, the Seventh Level Engagement Framework is a tool to measure your success in connecting with others. Your Seventh Level Statement reflects your own values and beliefs.

Before you can walk through this framework and reach the Seventh Level with someone else, you have to determine your own Seventh Level Statement. You have to establish what the holy grail of engagement looks like for you. You need to know who you are and what you stand for. What are your core values and mission? What do you believe in? What do you want to communicate to the world? That is your Seventh Level Statement. Start by writing your statement. Once you know what you stand for, use it as the lens to communicate with your customers and employees from Level One through the Seventh Level.

Identifying your values is a mandatory first step before you can meaningfully connect with your audience. Only when you know your own narrative can you work toward getting others to engage with you at the highest level.

So start by asking yourself the following questions:

- Who are you?
- What do you stand for?
- What do you believe in?
- Why do you do what you do?

I'm a pop culture junkie, so let's look at some examples from some of my favorite fictional characters. All of these characters have strong personal values and beliefs that they use as a compass in connecting meaningfully with others, which builds a loyal following to make a significant impact. (And isn't that what we all want?)

We all love Star Wars, right? (Or at least, I do.) One of Luke Skywalker's core beliefs was that there was good in the world despite the darkness. This shaped him and was the lens through which he made the decisions he made on his journey.

For you younger readers, maybe you're a bigger Harry Potter fan. Harry deeply believed he should protect both his own magical community and the nonmagic world from forces of evil at all costs. That was his Seventh Level.

And for you comic book fans, T'Challa (aka Black Panther) valued community and family connection.

Each of these characters felt their sense of purpose pulsing through them, but each needed guidance to understand how to access it. Their sense of purpose stemmed from their Seventh Level Statement.

Each of them also had a guide—Yoda, Dumbledore, and Okoye (Danai Gurira), respectively—to help them on their personal journey. After you've identified your Seventh Level, let this framework be your guide, teaching you to connect with others, and leverage your inner purpose—the thing that makes you, you.

Each of the characters mentioned also had a loyal following of people that supported them in accomplishing their goals. You, too, are probably looking for loyal friends and followers to help you build your business.

Sticking with pop culture, don't be like Julia Roberts's character in *Runaway Bride*. She was a chameleon with each romantic interest, and every time a date asked her how she liked her eggs cooked, she gave a different answer! She finally established her personal Seventh Level at the end of the movie with the help of her guide (Richard Gere) and realized that she could love herself and also be in a relationship. When you go through the framework without knowing your own personal Seventh Level, you end up changing yourself all of the time for your customers and employees, which means you'll wind up having poached eggs one day, scrambled the next, and over easy the day after that—and you'll never perfect any one recipe.

AVOID THE "UNCLE SNAPTIME" TRAP

When you don't know your own Seventh Level, you end up trying to be something you're not. It's like that uncle at the barbecue who is trying to be cool while talking to the younger kids and says, "Hey, are you on SnapTime?" They look at him like, umm, do you mean Snapchat or FaceTime? He thinks he's being cool; they think he's inauthentic. Unfortunately, I'm aging out as well. Not that long ago as a teacher, I was trying to connect to my millennial and Gen Z students. Rather than trying to step outside of my comfort zone and pretend I was like them in terms of the music they listened to or the movies they watched, I asked them what they loved to read, since I genuinely do love to read just about anything. I ended up reading the *Twilight* series (before any of my adult friends even knew what *Twilight* was) so I could keep my finger on the pulse of their pop culture in a way that felt authentic to me. As a teacher, learning and reading were aligned with connecting with them. If I had tried to listen to the same music or watch the same TV shows they did, or DM them on Instagram, they would have sent me the eye-roll emoji, thinking I was a loser or a tryhard. Instead, I used my Seventh Level Statement—to inspire and educate. I was inspired by what they were learning, reading, and excited by, and found a way to connect with them as a person and a reader.

Marketing today focuses on authenticity, but—like engagement—few marketers know what that really means. It's not about trying to be like another generation. For example, an older, fast food restaurant, with a demographic of baby boomers decides to use teen slang on its Twitter account as a failed attempt to "talk like millennials" ends up looking tone-deaf and out of touch. This is not being aligned with your personal Seventh Level Statement and not communicating that statement so that others understand what you believe in. Big brands always tell me how they are trying to connect with millennials and Gen Z, and generations who are not even born yet. I always like to note that besides these trendy new generations, there are groups that need to continue to be acknowledged (like Baby Boomers and Gen X) that I have coined as the *millennial-minded*. Because while we have all become obsessed with millennials as a demographic, millennials as a whole have impacted other generations in a psychographic way. When a big brand does not know why they are trying to connect with a specific demographic and they make snap decisions to keep up with the trends without acknowledging their own Seventh Level Statement, their attempts to connect fail. They don't know who *they* are, and so they focus on the markets they're trying to reach instead of communicating their own beliefs and values to different markets. Millennials, Gen Z, and millennial-minded customers see through the brands' misaligned attempts at authenticity and roll their eyes.

You should know what you believe in first, then connect with the people who resonate with that stated belief. When you're driven by your Seventh Level Statement and can communicate it clearly, you reach multiple audiences through an authentic lens, eventually connecting with them at the Seventh Level. That lens allows you to think about the next generation without abandoning existing customers.

Have you seen the movie *The Intern*? In the film, Robert de Niro is a bored, retired executive who takes a job at a startup run by Anne Hathaway. He comes to work in a suit and tie and carries a leather briefcase as he did for his entire career. He's curious about his young coworkers but doesn't try to be like them. He offers advice from another generation and solves both some personal and business situations during the film, saving the day when Anne Hathaway comes into her own as the CEO she's meant to be.

My dad—who LOVES that film—is in his sixties and is helping me build my company. He doesn't try to be a millennial. He just is who he is. He's had to change the *way* that he communicates (Level Two: Unsystematic Engagement—more on that later) with us because he's old school, Wall Street, and we're all millennials and Gen Zers. He's had to soften up a bit with his delivery of what he believes in, but he hasn't pretended to be something that he's not. His wisdom and insight offer more value to me than if he tried to be like everyone else who works for the company. I wanted to work with him because he is different. His Seventh Level Statement is always adding value to the work he produces, and this is what he does for me at CatalystCreativ. His Seventh Level aligned with my Seventh Level in the fact that he wants to add value to helping to build CatalystCreativ via the intention to inspire and educate others. We want to put out work that adds value, has integrity, is quality, and teaches people about how to better their business.

Once you identify what you stand for, you can then go through the framework knowing how to leverage who you are to connect with others. If you don't first identify your Seventh Level Statement, you keep changing yourself to reflect what everyone else thinks you are, and that's not sustainable.

As a company, identifying your core beliefs and values is instrumental in ensuring your organization meets its employee, sales, marketing, and relationship goals. This most often appears as a mission statement but can also be a tagline that drives the company's decisions.

For Nike, for example, it's "Just do it." Or more recently, "Believe in something, even if it means sacrificing everything."

For Apple, it's "Think different."

For Harley-Davidson, it's "All for freedom. Freedom for all."

Each of these statements should drive the decision-making and engagement for each brand in their internal and external decisions. They know who they are, they know what their values are, and if they make sure to live by their Seventh Level, they will continue to be successful with their audience.

MY PERSONAL SEVENTH LEVEL

My personal Seventh Level incorporates building connections while inspiring and educating others. This has always been within me and I have used it in many different aspects of my career.

In short, I believe that everyone has the right to be inspired. I am curious about people and believe each person has the capability to be inspired and activated in their own lives if someone just takes time to get to know them and reach them where they are.

I choose to inspire because when I am doing these things, I add meaning and value to my life. It's impacted my perception of the brands I personally interact with—they need to somehow teach me or better me as a human being. And when I engage this way, I know I'm engaging at my own Seventh Level.

RECOGNIZING YOUR SEVENTH LEVEL

My Seventh Level Statement is the driving force that guides me throughout my life that allows me to connect with others. As I mentioned, my Seventh Level Statement is to inspire and connect with people.

As I look back on my life experiences, I was driven to make sure everyone felt included. I've always cared about building community and connections. When I was three years old, I lined up my stuffed animals on the stairs and sang "Party for Friends" every day. My mom recalls walking into the lunchroom when I was in first grade to see me making sure every person in the class was included at the lunch table. I ensured that one kid traded Doritos for another kid's Dunkaroos, facilitating connections between them. I wanted everyone to feel seen, heard, and loved—and sometimes that desire took the shape of brokering fair snack exchanges!

During my time as an educator, I was passionate about getting to know each and every one of my students, about understanding where they come from and their values and beliefs.

Connection has always been extremely important to me. Even though I left the education field, I still educate and inspire. My Seventh Level Statement guided me to a different career, but I kept teaching, it just so happened to be in a different field. I found myself going from building community and connection in a classroom to doing the same thing in hospitality, in events, and in marketing. I found that I am still me wherever I am, whether it be the traditional classroom, a restaurant, or a burgeoning neighborhood like Downtown Las Vegas (a story for later in this book).

Across all these experiences, I've found that in order to

connect with different types of people from different walks of life, I've needed to understand where they were coming from, what they believed in, and what mattered most to them.

Now it's your turn.

WHAT'S YOUR SEVENTH LEVEL STATEMENT?

Take a moment to look back on your life and think about an experience when you most felt like yourself. Why did you feel so fulfilled and self-actualized in that moment? Your answer to these questions might lead you to your Seventh Level Statement—the guiding force behind the decisions you make and how you engage. We each have our own individual Seventh Level as a person or as a business. That's where you ultimately want to engage with your customers. To do that, however, you have to start with yourself.

Take the time to assess your Seventh Level Statement—both for yourself individually and for your company—because defining your own Seventh Level Statement is the only way for you to know when you've actually reached the Seventh Level with someone else.

During my presentations, I always give my audience a moment or two to think of what their Seventh Level Statement is, and then to share it with a colleague or the person sitting next to them.

I'd like to do the same for you. Take a moment right now to think about your personal Seventh Level Statement. (You could also try this out now for your brand or company, but the examples below are all personal Seventh Level Statements.)

Allow me to share some examples. The following are various Seventh Level Statements from people who attended the 2019 AMA Triangle High Five Conference and shared them on social media:

My Seventh Level is getting more accurate, clinically validated healthcare information online to aid people managing their own care.

Going off the beaten path to discover stories of ordinary people who are taking unique and extraordinary journeys.

My Seventh Level is my creative freedom.

Providing peace of mind to clients' pain points is my Seventh Level.

My Seventh Level is to entertain the people I connect with in a unique and intriguing fashion.

Authenticity = my Seventh Level.

New companies need to take the time to figure out their mission statement and values. I've seen many new companies with massive valuations grow and expand rapidly only to then fail because they should have really taken a step back and decided what they stand for first before selling it to everyone else. Once they've determined their Seventh Level Statement, then they can move forward to sell something, build a relationship with their customers, and hire support.

HOW MY SEVENTH LEVEL LED ME TO DOWNTOWN VEGAS

My position in the hospitality industry fostered building connections, but over time it didn't speak enough to the education part of my interests. As such, I started to feel limited in the hospitality industry space. I was always looking for ways to inspire, engage, *and* educate—I wanted to use my Seventh Level. I created a nonprofit event series, produced a nonprofit music festival in Central Park, organized a TEDx, and helped produce the Summit Series Entrepreneurship Conference on a cruise ship—all while having a full-time job. I was trying to explore my Seventh Level Statement while still financially supporting myself. After producing that Summit Series event at sea, the team asked me to produce a similar Summit Series event in Lake Tahoe, California.

And that's where I met the CEO of Zappos, Tony Hsieh. Through a series of coincidences and slightly embarrassing faux pas (you can read the full story on the About the Author pages at the end of the book), I ended up having a conversation with Tony about what I wanted to do with my life. We found that our Seventh Level Statements collided on several key points. Our Seventh Level Statements also crossed with that of my best friend, Robert Fowler, who wanted to be able to use his understanding of experiences to beautify the world. Robert and I founded our brand consulting firm, and Tony provided some initial seed funding.

We wanted to call ourselves something that would signify our unique approach to marketing and experiences, so we decided to name the company CatalystCreativ. *Catalyst* because our intention was to inspire (catalyze) formerly passive consumers to active participants in their own lives. And *Creativ* because through this inspiration, we help others identify the creativity that lies dormant within them.

Our first client was the relaunch of Downtown Las Vegas, a $350 million revitalization initiative that Tony was focused on after Zappos, which had recently been acquired by Amazon. Tony and I wanted to create experiences that would inspire those who lived in Downtown Vegas, and so we launched Catalyst Week, a free event designed to give residents access to thirty inspirational thought leaders who traveled from all over the world to come to Vegas and speak for free. These were the sort of influential people who typically spoke in places like New York and San Francisco but rarely in Downtown Las Vegas. The event was a massive success.

Over these immersive couple of days in Downtown Vegas, the speakers thought they were coming to learn more about Downtown Vegas, but they ended up learning more about themselves. Many found their Seventh Level Statements. One attendee, Dan Fredinburg, wrote to me after the event:

> I planned to write you very soon myself to thank you for inviting me. I've really appreciated the opportunity that the downtown project provides; and even more importantly, I've gotten to spend time with an amazing cast of people who are all here because of you. I really meant what I said about cherishing the opportunity to learn from some of the most selfless and vibrant people in the world. They, and you, make me a better person. I'm excited to be a loyal friend and collaborator with all of you to ensure that a huge, tangible and measurable impact is made in a fashion that so directly makes the world a better place.

Thank you for finding a way to inspire a robot,

Dan

Dan was one of the catalysts who made me realize I was doing exactly what I was supposed to be doing. I wasn't simply introducing people to a city or to each other. I was introducing people to a part of themselves they may not have known before (their own personal Seventh Level).

Catalyst Week was a huge success with a massive waiting list. While Catalyst Week focused on entrepreneurs and business leaders, we launched Creativ Week to focus on creatives to meet the demands of all of the people who wanted to participate in this experience but who didn't necessarily fall into the target audience for Catalyst Week.

For both events, we created experiences for people to identify their own Seventh Level and connect from that place. We started every week by asking people to share what they wanted to be when they were eight years old. Just like my students on the rug, we asked these people to share not what they do but who they are. We asked what drove and inspired them before they had bills to pay or before their parents had told them they had to be something. We told them we wanted them to come from that childhood mind where they wanted to be professional basketball players, astronauts, professional singers, and sometimes all three. We wanted them to connect with each other from that creative, inspired place. Over the course of two and a half years, we curated two thousand thought leaders to participate in our experience and educate and inspire the Downtown Vegas community.

Attendees left saying, "My life just changed!" or "I met my husband!" or "I received funding!" or "Thank you for this incredible opportunity!"

We had created a Seventh Level experience: a place where individuals could connect with themselves and each other from a place of personal values and beliefs. Presenters gave Catalyst Week talks to the public, with a prompt that encouraged them to share not what they do but who they are, and recall a moment in time that acted as a catalyst for them. They not only inspired thousands of others to see themselves differently but they left feeling inspired and connected because they were given a space to share from a place of authenticity. They were connecting in a way that was meaningful, emotional, and visceral. It was much more than a normal networking conference, and it was a huge moment for me as well. I realized for the first time that this was an opportunity to combine my understanding of events, marketing, branding, and education, and to redefine what ROI looked like for the world. Sure, I could help people boost their return on investments, but just as importantly, I could create a *new form of ROI: "Ripple Of Impact."*

A lot of people attending these experiences had companies of their own or worked for large Fortune 100 brands, and when they felt that special something, they wanted to know how we could do the same thing for them. Since that first Catalyst Week in 2012, we ended up applying our Seventh Level secret sauce to the work we have done with other brands, helping them on branding, experiential, and marketing campaigns to increase engagement and build meaningful connections in the same way we did in Downtown Vegas but now all over the country and the world.

FAST-FORWARD TO TODAY

Seventh Level Statements make people who they are, and if they can't bring their Seventh Level selves to work, then they don't feel fulfilled. I want to give everyone the opportunity to bring their whole selves to work, which I believe they deserve to do. I want them to align their personal values and beliefs to the workplace. I've always believed that everyone has the right to feel like they can connect with each other in the world.

At CatalystCreativ, we do a lot of different things that allow us to create a culture that embodies our Seventh Level, which is to activate passive consumers into active participants. One simple thing we do is a weekly check-in where we talk about what's going on in our "personal" lives outside of work. We share who we are, not just what we are doing. We share what's driving us and how it's impacting our work.

Today, I help and inspire people to connect their brands with their customers. I believe that we all deserve to live a life filled with purpose and impact. I believe that the interactions we have with people should be intentional. At CatalystCreativ, we essentially use our understanding of engagement to activate customers—internal or external—to care about themselves, each other, and the world around them.

WORKING THROUGH THE SEVEN LEVELS

Once you determine your Seventh Level Statement, you, too, can use our secret sauce to create meaningful, engaged relationships with the people in your life—your employees and your customers, for sure, but also your partner, family, and friends.

But you can't simply jump from Level One to the Seventh Level, especially with someone new to you or your brand. You can't expect a customer to immediately engage with you on a high level. You have to build trust first. You wouldn't marry someone if you didn't know anything about them. If you were asking someone to make a lasting commitment to you, you'd first identify what you stand for, then take the time to get to know them, and then ask for their commitment. You'd want to build a relationship with them before saying, "I do."

It's the same in business.

Everyone strives to be more like Nike and Apple. These companies have a solid, concrete identity. How can you do the same? The first step is establishing your Seventh Level Statement, which requires knowing who you are and what you believe in.

As you bring people from Level One to Level Six, striving toward engagement at the Seventh Level, your audience becomes more connected to your message, action, or a request. These meaningful relationships lead to greater customer and employee loyalty, achievement, productivity, and sales, among other benefits. By understanding the level where the person you're communicating with currently stands, it helps you determine the best next steps for engaging with them to take them to the next level.

Next, we will dive into Phase 1: Attract. The bottom three levels of the Seventh Level Engagement Framework in this phase center on earning trust. In order to build a meaningful relationship with anyone, you need to show that you are taking the time, energy, and effort to get to know them as a human, not just as a number.

PART TWO

PHASE 1: ATTRACT

Chapter Two

LEVEL ONE: DISENGAGEMENT

YOU'RE BORING

You can learn a lot by watching Nora Ephron's 1989 cinematic magnum opus, *When Harry Met Sally...*

First-time viewers will discover where the phrase "I'll have what she's having" originated. Younger rom-com aficionados will receive a crash course in late 1980s style, shoulder pads and all. And if you sort of ignore the film's final scene, the movie answers the age-old question: "Can men and women truly be friends?" (Answer: Yes.)

But what you might not have noticed at first pass is that this romantic saga about two star-crossed strangers-turned-enemies-turned-friends-turned-enemies-turned-lovers does a phenomenal job of demonstrating the Seventh Level Engagement Framework. The film offers great examples of each level of engagement, so throughout the following chapters, I'll be highlighting scenes from the film to showcase each level on the Seventh Level Engagement Framework, starting with Level One: Disengagement.

Harry Burns (played by Billy Crystal) and Sally Albright (portrayed by Meg Ryan) first meet as freshly minted University of Chicago graduates during a long, shared car ride to New York City, where their new jobs have taken them. Off the bat, they don't get along, but they have a long drive ahead of them, and someone needs to come up with a plan. Sally takes the initiative and dives in.

"I have it all figured out," she says. "It's an eighteen-hour trip which breaks down into six shifts of three hours each, or alternatively we could break it down by mileage."

She's put in a lot of time, energy, and effort to plan out the trip so both parties share in the workload.

"There's a map on the visor that I've marked to show the locations where we can change shifts," Sally continues.

While she's talking and explaining her thoughtful plan, Harry is climbing into the back seat of the car to get snacks.

"Grapes?" he offers to her, without actually hearing a word she said. His mind was focused on those snacks.

Level One is characterized by a person showing disinterest—and disinterest is just what Harry exhibits the second Sally tries to strike up a conversation about how they'll divvy up the driving responsibilities. Harry is disengaged from Sally, not listening, not responding, and not appreciating the work she put into planning the trip.

Harry is at Level One: Disengagement.

THIS IS BORING, BUT THERE IS HOPE!

When someone is stuck in Level One, they are disinterested. They're bored. They're idle with their work. They're avoiding tasks, interactions, or attempts at communication. Oftentimes, there is little to no emotional response. This sort of engagement happens frequently in the early stages of any type of relationship.

Picture a first-grade classroom full of six-year-old students. When the teacher says, "Raise your hand if you're in first grade," you'd expect everyone to raise their hand. Well, except for the disengaged child, staring blankly out the window, ignoring the question.

People at this level in relation to you, your company, or your brand might be thinking, "This is boring."

But don't fret—there is hope!

Disengagement is not the opposite of engagement; it's merely a level of engagement. Even if someone is disengaged, the good news is that they're not apathetic. This framework is not to blame someone else for being disengaged but to look at what you can do better to connect with them.

The framework is a ladder that allows you to climb from one level to the next. At each level, you improve your communication with your audience, thereby increasing the attention they give you and deepening the connection you have with them.

So what can you do to move someone to Level Two?

You're going to need to establish a game plan. To determine why your audience is at Level One, ask yourself what you are doing wrong. Something is wrong with how you're engaging with them, so you must identify the problem in order to fix it. If it's not immediately obvious what is wrong, start by asking yourself a series of questions.

· Who are you talking to?

- How are you talking to them?
- Where are you talking to them?

Let's take a look at the following examples.

IN EXTERNAL CUSTOMERS

As we discussed initially, you should be using your Seventh Level Statement as the lens through which you go through the framework with others. The framework allows you to take ownership of your own communication and connection to better your relationship with others versus blaming others. At this level (and all levels), it's important to not try to be something you are not. As I mentioned earlier in the book, in marketing, we talk a lot about "authenticity," which is where your Seventh Level Statement comes in. You are not going to be who your customers want you to be, but rather you are going to identify what customers reflect and connect with who you are. In other words, once you know who your customers are, you can connect with them by being who you are, not being who they want you to be.

This engagement framework allows you to think about how to engage and connect with your customers in an all-encompassing, 360-degree way. It can be used across every touchpoint from employee relations to digital and social media marketing, to physical events and experiences, to graphic design, and brand identity that includes your logo, website, and design. At Level One, your audience doesn't respond to your efforts, whether it's an invitation to an event, a new product announcement, or a social media post. Disengagement with your external customers shows up in a variety of ways. Perhaps you send out a survey in an email to three hundred subscribers, but you barely receive any completed surveys. Maybe you post a photo on Instagram but only get a few likes or no likes at all. Or you've planned a huge industry convention, but hardly any attendees have made their way over to the main stage where a keynote you thought was going to be a hit is flopping.

You have to ask yourself if you're sending the invitation the way your audience best receives it. For example, do they use snail mail or email? Have you announced your product in the channels they frequent? Do they use the same social media platform as you do?

The beauty of online communication is having access to real-time data and metrics. If you see that only a small percentage of people have clicked on your Facebook ad, for example, clearly, the ad is not working. It's time to switch it up!

Online communication gives us the flexibility to try things, change things, and find what works. Treat this as a learning process. Try running two ads for the same thing on two different platforms to see which one gets better traction. With a bit of trial and error, you can learn how to change, evolve, and pivot from what is *not* working and begin to identify what *is* working. What is the best platform to reach your audience? The answer to that is an ongoing process of research and testing.

Perhaps you are in the design department and you are thinking about creating a new logo or brand identity. Do not just change your logo to reflect what you think a new generation of potential customers wants; do what you feel best communicates your Seventh Level Statement. Dunkin' Donuts changed their name to Dunkin' in early 2019. They thought very intentionally when determining their new brand. They did not change who they were, their colors, or the font their audience knows and loves. They just cleaned it up and shortened the name to reflect what they always stood for. If Dunkin' decided to create a sleek black font that had nothing to do with its brand identity because that was what "modern, trendy brands are doing these days," you better believe people would be outraged and very disengaged.

To move your customers out of Level One disengagement, ask yourself the following questions:

- Do I know who my customer is? Where she lives, her profession, her age, her interests?
- What tools do my customers use?
- What time of day are they using the tools?
- How am I targeting them?
- Am I using visual and/or direct copy marketing language which will pique my customers' interest?

Whether you are creating a branding or marketing campaign or inviting people to attend an experience, these questions matter because it allows you to know who your customer is. You can find the answers to these questions through market research in the form of online surveys or reaching out to previous customers. Ask them what you did right and what you did wrong so that you can learn and then pivot. Apply growth hacking methodologies to help gain insight with your customer experimentation across marketing, development, and sales to determine the most efficient ways to capture audience attention and grow your business. One method would be creating a message, testing it with an audience that you have identified as your customer, seeing how they respond, and then iterating and retesting that message until your conversion point is most optimal (and your target audience is highly refined).

Because you have already identified what *you* stand for (see the previous chapter), now it's time to target who you *think* your customers are. Then you optimize, test, pivot, and make sure you're converting at a very low-cost point. If it's not working, you continue to pivot. If you're stuck on something that's not serving you, you're likely talking to the wrong people.

WHY ISN'T YOUR STRATEGY WORKING?

We use a practice at CatalystCreativ within this framework that we call Actions, Questions, Goals. For each level, we've identified an action that's associated with the level, a question that arises from that action, and a goal to get to the next level. For example, at Level One you want to identify the target audience that would care about your product—if you were able to engage them.

The first step on the path toward moving past Level One onto Level Two is to identify an action associated with Level One: Disengagement. For example, nobody is clicking on my Instagram ad.

The second step is to ask questions associated with the action:

- Does my target audience use Instagram?
- Who is my target audience?
- Where do they like to be spoken to?
- What time of day is best to communicate with them?

The third step is to test ads on multiple platforms and assess the results. When someone stops answering you— that is disengagement.

In each chapter, I've provided an example of the action, questions, goals we've developed for a sample company's marketing efforts (for their external customers) and also of a sample company's employee engagement efforts (for their internal customers).

For the external customer examples, I've used a fictional online mattress company as a sample case study that our team has analyzed and assessed on our own, using the framework, for this book. For the purposes of this example, this fictional company's Seventh Level Statement is, "We believe that great sleep is the fuel that drives all of us." At the end of the book, you'll find the complete case studies. You can fill out your own worksheet at The-SeventhLevel.com so you, too, can use this tool to reach the engagement you want at each level and move your internal and external customers up to the Seventh Level.

ACTION, QUESTIONS, GOALS:
EXTERNAL CUSTOMERS

ACTION

The Online Mattress Company runs a series of Instagram ads to drive traffic to their website. The audience is scrolling past the ads without clicking.

QUESTIONS

- What do their current customers look like?
- Where does their target audience spend time online?
- Are their ads on the right platform?
- Are they targeting the right audience?

GOALS

- Evaluate existing customer base.
- Identify the top two "types" of current customers that most often purchase.
- Identify one to two "types" of aspirational customers that they'd like to target.

The Online Mattress Company's goal is to use existing customer or aspirational target customer data to create personas that guide future ad targeting. The research focuses on demographics and psychographics, including where that "type" of person spends time, what they read, how they consume information, what social channels they use most, etc.

WITH YOUR INTERNAL CUSTOMER: IN THE WORKPLACE

As an employer, you want productivity from your employees, but if you don't identify what works best for them regarding how they like to be communicated to, you are making your job harder. From my perspective as an employer, you work for your employees. It is your job to create an environment that sets them up for success so they can help make the company a success.

If you find your employees unresponsive or flippant in their responses to your questions or requests, they are disengaged. Don't despair, however, you can turn things around by sitting them down, asking questions, and actively listening.

Set up structures for individualized communication and determine their preferred method of communication. Perhaps it's email or text or Slack. Set working communication hours. Perhaps they go to the gym at night or have family time on the weekends and don't want to be interrupted outside of the work hours that you have communicated. You can't expect immediate follow-up on a Sunday morning if you never established those as working hours from the beginning.

With an employee, ask yourself:

- What's my employee's preferred method of communication?
- What hours does my employee communicate?
- What tone am I using?

It comes back to getting to know the person, where they like to be spoken to, and how you can speak to them. It is crucial to take ownership as a manager/leader/director to identify what you can do better to communicate with your employees. From there, you can try to speak to them at a different time and place to see if the disengagement begins to shift.

ACTION, QUESTIONS, GOALS: INTERNAL CUSTOMERS

ACTION
An HR representative sends out an email to all employees requesting their participation in a new goal-setting program. The employees do not respond to the representative's email.

QUESTIONS
- Have they asked what their employees' preferred method of contact is?
- What time of day did they send the email?
- Did the HR representative send the email to a group or to each individual?

- Was the email successfully delivered to each employee?
- Have they tried reaching out to their employees personally to do an informal survey to ask why they didn't respond?

GOALS

- Establish company-wide communication guidelines and let employees know that they should expect to receive HR requests via email.
- Include links to information and resources related to each request and call them out in the message.
- When an employee is onboarded, ask what their preferred method of communication is.
- Send a follow-up to individual team members via their preferred contact method with a personal message to ensure they saw the original email.
- Set up a tracking tool to see who/when emails have been received and opened.

The HR representative's goal is to establish clear expectations around how and when employees will be receiving HR-related messages, so that employees are familiar with the process. The HR representative should also take on the responsibility of ensuring employees are familiar with the means through which they receive information and requests and understand when it's important to respond.

MOVING ON FROM LEVEL ONE

At Level One, your audience may not even know you exist. Your communications pass by them without response, and they don't notice because they're bored and disengaged. You must identify who and where they are. With that information, you can move on to Level Two and begin to think about how to communicate with them.

Chapter Three

———

LEVEL TWO: UNSYSTEMATIC ENGAGEMENT

I'M CONFUSED

While driving across the country together, Harry and Sally argue about whether men and women can just be friends. They don't understand one another, and they aren't speaking the same language.

"What I'm saying," Harry says, "and this is not a come-on in any way, shape, or form—is that men and women can't be friends because the sex part always gets in the way."

Sally disagrees and says she has a number of male friends and there is no sex involved.

"No man can be friends with a woman that he finds attractive," Harry continues. "He always wants to have sex with her."

Sally doesn't believe him. The discussion continues, and Sally finally tells Harry that it's too bad they can't be friends, then, as he's the only person she knows in New York.

Level Two is characterized by a person's confusion about the messaging. In the case of Harry and Sally, their personalities and philosophies on life (sex) are so different that they don't see eye to eye or understand one another. It wasn't that Sally was disengaged. They were talking to each other, but they weren't speaking the same language—all the while George and Ira Gershwin's "Let's Call the Whole Thing Off" ("You like tomato; I like tomahto") plays in the background.

I DON'T REALLY GET WHAT YOU'RE SAYING...

Have you ever browsed a grocery store aisle and picked up a new item that looked yummy, but when you turned it over and saw ninety ingredients that you couldn't pronounce, you immediately put it down out of sheer confusion?

Welcome to Level Two: Unsystematic Engagement.

I often see Level Two as a particularly huge issue in marketing. Companies often use jargon that no one understands, and then they're surprised when customers don't want to buy anything from them. Or they want to communicate that they are a fresh and clean brand but choose colors that remind someone of McDonald's. This is the importance of creating clear, concise messaging even with branding. You need to do the work to ensure the message you put out in the world is aligned with your Seventh Level lens and that your brand identity communicates what you are trying to convey.

Otherwise, customers might find themselves thinking, "I don't get what you're saying."

When we produced Catalyst Week, we had fifty people from different locations with busy lives on different schedules coming to participate in a three-day experience in a part of Las Vegas they probably knew nothing about. Talk about unsystematic engagement! We had to ensure that we clearly communicated everything about the experience. We sent out an email with all of the details, had a landing page with all details, and even sent videos—with, yes, the details! We sent reminders the day before and had printouts in the rooms. We made sure we were clearly communicating our asks and what they should expect when attending.

This is the importance of creating clear, concise messaging even with branding. You need to do the work to ensure the message you put out in the world is aligned with your Seventh Level lens and that your brand identity communicates what you are trying to convey.

When you reach Level Two, you need to clarify your communication. You know *who* you are talking to and *how* you're talking to them from Level One. Now it's time to make sure you're using the right words to connect with them clearly. Level One is *where* you say something and *to whom*, Level Two is *what* you say.

In personal relationships, whether with an employee, coworker, or family member, unsystematic engagement often looks like yelling at one another or talking over one another because we feel we are right. There's a sense of misunderstanding and, therefore, disinterest in the other point of view. You don't have to agree with someone and their viewpoint, but if you work to understand it, you can speak from a place of mutual respect.

The emotions indicative of unsystematic engagement consist of inadequacy, insecurity, and confusion. When someone feels these emotions, they're more likely to simply give up, move on, and drop down to Level One. The person you're trying to talk to—whether it be a client, an employee, or a partner—might be confused by your messaging. This means you need to change your perspective in order to connect with them in a meaningful way. Let's look at each audience in more detail.

Let's go back to using the Seventh Level Statement as a lens. When thinking about what you are saying to your customers, you are not going to speak like them, you are going to speak like you but in a way they understand. Perhaps you have multiple customer personas with different age ranges and different demographic data. You don't change who you are each time you speak to them; you think about what you stand for, and then you reframe it to communicate to the audience you are talking to. I would use very different words about what CatalystCreativ does to a millennial employee than I would to a "millennial-minded" client.

When my ninety-five-year-old grandma asks me what I do for work, I tell her, "I am in advertising and throw events." But I tell millennial colleagues that "I create strategic, creative marketing campaigns that increase engagement using an engagement framework I developed."

I am not changing our identity in the process. I am not trying to speak like my audience. I am still me. I'm just making sure that I'm clearly heard by aligning my messaging with my audience's understanding of the topic. Effective communication comes from another person understanding what you actually mean. So often, we speak in silos, thinking everyone gets what we are saying. If we put ourselves in the shoes of our different customer personas, but stay true to ourselves, our communication can guide us to connect more deeply with the people we care about.

IN EXTERNAL CUSTOMERS

Unsystematic engagement happens when your message is unclear and others don't understand who you are, what you do, or what you mean. It happens when you don't clearly communicate the purpose of your company, the value that it brings, and the benefits it offers. Or you neglect to explain the ingredients that make up your product, how exactly you go about your services, or the jargon you're using.

All of this translates to a customer not making a purchase or engaging with you in the desired way out of sheer confusion.

Customers at this level have no idea what you are marketing or selling to them. They arrive at your website, but they leave without making a transaction. They don't know what you want from them.

In order to avoid any confusion, it's imperative that you identify how to communicate to your customer in clear, concise language that's digestible. Refer back to the personas you created (for Level One) to determine who your target audience is and use them to evaluate how you should speak to those audience segments (for Level Two).

At this level, you should be surveying your customers to understand the language they *do* understand. Do a competitive analysis as well as possibly create a "brain trust" of potential customers to act as a sounding board for you. For example, when NPR was trying to reach more millennials, I became a founding board member of something called NPR Gen Listen, a board of millennials that would help guide them on how to clearly communicate their Seventh Level Statement in a way that felt authentic to millennials. At Level Two, you don't change who you are, you clearly communicate what you stand for in a way that is easy to understand.

A good rule of thumb: if you can't explain to an eight-year-old what you do, then your target customer probably won't get it either.

You want everyone from age eight to eighty to understand exactly what you're selling.

ACTION, QUESTIONS, AND GOALS:
EXTERNAL CUSTOMERS

ACTION

A potential customer for the Online Mattress Company visits their website after clicking on an ad, but they are confused by the process of purchasing a mattress online. The customer leaves the company's website without getting past the home page.

QUESTIONS

- Is the company clearly communicating the steps of buying and installing a mattress purchased online?
- How is the mattress company communicating the benefits of purchasing with them and buying a mattress online versus in-store to their potential customers?
- Has the company tested their messaging about the process of buying a mattress online?

GOALS

- Surveyed target audiences understand what their questions and barriers to entry to purchasing a mattress online are.
- Add messaging to the home page that makes it easy to understand the purchase journey for a customer and the value it provides by testing a variety of messaging tools (i.e., visually, video, copy) and see what performs best.
- Review competitor websites and messaging to analyze what messaging they're using to gather insight.

For the Online Mattress Company trying to attract customers who have never shopped online for a mattress before, at this level, a goal would be to demystify that experience. One way to do this would be preemptively alleviating any concerns and answering any questions a first-time buyer might have. They should spell out, step by step, what to expect from purchase to setup on their home page as well as incorporate key messaging that highlights the value of choosing this type of direct-to-consumer mattress over a traditional one. These actions are key to helping capture the attention of those who reach their site while at the second level of engagement.

WITH YOUR INTERNAL CUSTOMERS: IN THE WORKPLACE

In Levels One and Two, employees often worry they'll make a bad impression if they don't understand something. It's important to keep other people's feelings in mind. After explaining something, for example, do you catch yourself saying, "Does that make sense?"

What's the standard, go-to, immediate response? "Yes," even if the employee really didn't understand. No one likes feeling dumb, so they'll avoid admitting it.

A better question to ask is, "Did I explain that correctly?" This approach takes the pressure off the employee and puts it back on you, the leader. When we are trying to make decisions for ourselves and only think about what we understand or what makes sense to us, we exist in an echo chamber. And if you're standing on the sun, you're blind. You get lost in the way you communicate and everything that makes sense to you. You might think you explained the information well, but people work in various ways, and you want to make sure you and your employees are on the same page.

As before, you want to build from the lens of your Seventh Level Statement. You're not changing who you are to accommodate each one of your employees. That would be exhausting! And unrealistic. Rather, since you know who you are and what you stand for, you're simply refining your communication to hit the right notes for the right people.

As a leader, it's also important to let your team know they can tell you if they don't understand something. They have to feel comfortable coming to you. The last thing you want is an employee nodding her head in agreement, going off to spend a week on a task, and then showing up with the opposite of what you asked. It delays the end product and leaves them feeling guilty or unintelligent for not understanding.

As I tell you a story about one of my favorite students, think about one of your employees or customers that may fit this description. Think about how you may just not understand where they are coming from, and if you took the time and energy to do so, their engagement would change dramatically.

As I mentioned earlier, back in my teaching days, I asked my students to sit on the rug during our morning meeting to talk about anything they wanted for one minute. Students were used to sharing about their personal lives and how it impacted them in the classroom. This led to a more open and welcoming atmosphere, which was crucial for developing trusting relationships with my students.

I noticed one of my brightest students struggling and that her approach to reading was growing apathetic. I didn't understand why she was in the lowest reading group but had one of the largest vocabularies in the class. Because of the morning meetings, when I asked her why she felt she was not doing well in reading, the trust was already built. She said she felt like she wasn't smart when she made mistakes and felt less inclined to keep trying as a result. She was a perfectionist, even at an early age.

I'm sure we all remember how challenging reading was in elementary school. You did your best to sound out the words you didn't know, right? In front of all your peers, no less! That's nerve-racking enough! We all know that in order to learn, you have to make mistakes, but because she was a perfectionist, any hiccup made her feel inadequate. I felt for her, as I remember moments that I felt similarly in my life, so I had empathy for her. I sat her down and talked about how we could make reading more approachable. I explained that no one knows how to sound out the words right away and that it takes practice. She communicated that it would be more fun to practice reading, and easier to grasp the words, if we turned our exercises into an art project. She loved hearts and was passionate about creativity, so we put the vocabulary words on hearts that we cut out together. The best way for her to engage with reading new words was to incorporate the words into something she felt a stronger connection to. The standard communication used for another student in the same reading group would not work for her no matter how hard I tried.

Reading practice became structured in a way she was better able to understand, so she felt more confident when approaching it. And this little girl looked forward to learning to read and busted out her heart-shaped index cards throughout the rest of the year. All it took was a personal connection to find a way to communicate information in a way she'd better understand. The following year, when I ran into her brother, he told me that she was taken out of the lower reading group altogether and placed in the highest reading group.

These are catalyst moments. If someone hadn't seen and

reached out to her in a way she understood, what would have happened?

After reading Steve Jobs's biography, I was inspired by the teacher who took him aside as a student who was acting up and invested in him rather than scolding him. He gave that teacher so much credit for helping him not lose confidence in himself. I tried to do that with every one of my students. Steve Jobs needed someone not only to notice him but also to talk to him in a way he understood, to communicate in a way that he could receive. Some of the highest-achieving people in the world, if communicated to in a language they don't understand, drop down from Level Two to Level One (disengagement) and would not have turned into the success stories we know and respect today.

I've been there, on the other side of the coin, desperately wanting to power through a task and hoping I get it right because I would feel stupid if I asked what my boss or teacher meant. That's why I make it abundantly clear at CatalystCreativ that the team can come to me anytime if they don't get something. Since I always have a lot going on in my mind, I talk fast, whether in person or online. I admit, sometimes I need structure. When I'm off the cuff and sending out emails, it's not the best thing for anyone, but we have created a culture where everyone feels very comfortable saying, "Amanda, I literally have no idea what you're talking about."

ACTION, QUESTIONS, GOALS:
INTERNAL CUSTOMERS

ACTION

Employees are confused about how to set up their new benefits accounts, so they do not enroll in the program.

QUESTIONS

- Did the benefits team adequately explain how the program will work for each employee? What format did they use (i.e., printed material, video, etc.)?
- Did they host a webinar or session or provide another opportunity to answer employee questions about how to enroll in the program?
- Did they explain the steps of how to enroll in the program in a simple and easily digestible email?
- Did the benefits team provide enough information and resources about the new plan (i.e., plan overview, link to provider website, phone number to speak to a plan representative, etc.)?

GOALS

- Send out links to program information and resources in a well-organized email and ask employees to share specific questions directly.
- Set clear and direct calls to action and deadlines in every email.

- When an action is required after a specific email, always add "Action Required" to the beginning of the subject line.
- Host a live webinar with employees to review the program and answer questions, then share a recording of that webinar with the whole staff via email.

For Level Two, the benefits team's goal is to ensure all potential gaps in understanding are filled through refined communication practices. They will develop clear, easy-to-understand messaging and leverage several communication tools to accommodate individuals who take in information differently, so all team members will clearly understand what's being offered to them and the steps to enroll.

At Level Two, we need to stop blaming others for a lack of connection. This is where we start internalizing and asking how we can grow and be better. I'm also building from the foundation I have already developed by going back and asking those first-level questions: Who am I speaking to? How am I speaking to them? What can I do better?

So as a leader, how can you be better? How can you communicate better? What tools can you use to clearly and concisely share with others? Imagine how dramatically the world would change if everyone said, "I'm so sorry I didn't properly communicate that to you. Let me take the time and energy to do what I need to for you to understand."

To resolve this, it's important to actively listen and speak in a way that others can understand. Moving up in levels requires you to say, "What do you hear, and what do you feel I'm trying to say?"

In the *When Harry Met Sally...* example at the start of this chapter, Sally could have delved into why Harry felt the way he did. She could put herself in his perspective to see it from the other side. But she didn't, remaining at Level Two.

Relationships—whether at work or outside of it—can all benefit from additional clarity of communication. My husband, my best friend, and my father all work with me at CatalystCreativ. (You can imagine, the Seventh Level is pervasive in my entire life!) Things that I've learned in my workplace I bring home with me; things from home come to work—especially since they work with me.

Sometimes, my husband and I repeat back what the other has said for clarification purposes. For example, there are times I say something, he repeats it back to me, and his interpretation is completely off from what I thought I'd made clear.

"That's not what I meant at all," I say.

This allows me to get perspective on what he heard in order for me to frame future conversations differently. Repeating after each other allow us to see if we're on the same page or maybe not in the same book at all.

If your workplace environment isn't set up to say, "I don't understand," you can paraphrase what you heard, "I just heard, blank blank blank," which gives the initial speaker the space to agree or correct. If you're having remote calls, put it in writing and then email them stating, "This is what we agreed to." Get creative! I worked for a boss years ago with whom I had frequent miscommunications. Often, after we had a meeting, I'd bring something up I thought he'd said, and he'd respond, "I didn't say that." Eventually I started taking word-for-word notes of what he'd say in our meetings and asked him to sign my notes before we left the office to ensure there wasn't a discrepancy between what was said and what was remembered. This might seem like a drastic measure, but situationally, it worked for my boss and me.

MOVING ON FROM LEVEL TWO

While social media is great for viral content and creating opportunities for people to spread messages rapidly to a large audience, it also has in some ways contributed to continued unsystematic engagement because it emphasizes short sound bites and quick responses. Oftentimes, people don't take the time to understand each other. They're stuck in their silos, yelling at one another because they think they're right. They don't take the time to identify the best way to communicate with those who might have different viewpoints.

Social media is also super-fast-paced, which doesn't allow someone to step back and formulate a response with care and respect. If we have the tools and an audience we are talking to, we have a responsibility to be thoughtful with our responses, our comments, and our posts, but this is easier said than done in the immediacy that comes with social media communication.

At Level Two, communication is a problem, so you need to assess why. Once you've identified who your audience is (Level One) and how to clearly communicate with them (Level Two), you can move to Level Three and make sure your audience doesn't feel frustrated by your communications.

Chapter Four

LEVEL THREE: FRUSTRATED ENGAGEMENT

I'M DISTRACTED

As the plot develops, Harry and Sally cross paths again, and an unlikely friendship begins to blossom, thanks to Harry being less of a jerk and Sally being a bit more open to a male friendship.

In a scene following the engagement of Sally's best friend to Harry's best friend, we spot the titular characters shopping for an engagement gift together at a gadget store. Harry eyes a karaoke machine and, along with Sally, begins to sing a rousing rendition of a duet from *Oklahoma!*

The chemistry between them is palpable, and they look like they're having a wonderful time—that is until Harry spots his ex-wife, Helen, and stops singing/interacting with Sally altogether.

Level Three is characterized by a person demonstrating interest, only to have that interest wane due to distraction.

WAIT, WHAT'S THAT OVER THERE?

Limit the distractions for your internal and external customers because the world is distracting enough. Remote work is on the rise—dogs (mine's barking as I write), children, and family members may be around. Open or closed workspaces: there are always distractions. How are we teaching employees to limit their distractions? How can we keep our customers' attention? Level Three is about boundaries.

As a marketer and someone who thinks about branding, I'm always a customer. I'm an anthropological engagement researcher in my own life. I'm a customer analyzing what brands could do differently, which gives me a certain self-awareness when I'm analyzing my own work for clients.

So many things can distract the people you're trying to engage with. Frustrated engagement happens all the time. Level Three encompasses the idea that you want to connect with an experience, but then you're distracted from it. You understand the message and have an intention to connect, but something draws your attention away. Hey, it happens! Perhaps it's the message itself, something to do with the company, or just being distracted by something happening in your life.

Take a six-year-old who is about to participate in a school project when a chirping bird lands on the windowsill. He is suddenly distracted. Or perhaps he's distracted because his parents are going through a divorce and his attention is continually pulled inward.

Or what about when you attend a charity event and are trying to listen to the speaker on stage talk about a very personal story, only to be asked by your waiter ten times if you'd like more water?

Ever watch a video on your phone or tablet and as soon as an ad pops up, rather than finishing the video, you just close out of the site altogether? This is frustrated engagement.

Personally, I hate when platforms do that. I recently watched a video on Facebook when suddenly an irrelevant ad began playing midway through that had no association with the content I was watching. "What the...?

I didn't want to see this!" This is the furthest thing away from connecting with a customer. It was a forced interaction and left me frustrated and annoyed instead of interested in learning more about the product. Advertisers think they're being clever by forcing people to watch their ads, but instead they're only irritating people and leaving a bad taste in their mouth. I ended up exiting out of the ad, which means I exited out of the video and never finished watching it.

My attention is valuable—as is yours and that of your audience. I am open to content that is relevant and connected to what I believe in and value. Let's go back to your Seventh Level Statement as a lens. If someone targeted me (Level One)—I am their customer—spoke to me in a way I understand (Level Two), and clearly communicated this to me in a way that made sense and did not create a distraction from what I was trying to achieve—i.e., the video was engaging and interesting and aligned with what I believe in and spoke to what they believe in—I would connect with them in a more meaningful way. Yes, it seems like a lot of work, but the other option is that customers constantly fall off because they have that annoyed taste in their mouth. As media properties, it is crucial to think about a proper advertising strategy. Do not pop up something in the middle of content that is irrelevant and annoying to the wrong audience.

The emotions indicative of frustrated engagement consist of frustration, annoyance, lack of control, and distraction.

Although we can't control everything (like those distracting midvideo ads!), we can control ourselves and the way we communicate. Let's take a look at what Level Three engagement looks like in our customers and our employees.

IN EXTERNAL CUSTOMERS

In a world filled with distractions, it's crucial to not create any more for our customers.

When a customer gets to your website, make sure it doesn't take too long to load. Or when a customer is asked to go to a landing page, make sure the pop-up you add to that page is relevant to what you're asking them to do and why they're there.

Social media in general leaves us distracted. You're building an audience in the sense of creating your own user funnel, but it's important to *use* the tools instead of letting the tools use you. If social media isn't employed in a way that pushes your customer base to a higher level of engagement by encouraging a specific targeted action, you're only hurting your messaging efforts.

The way to leverage tools to ensure limited distractions

is to build off of Levels One and Two, and then incorporate pop-ups, emails, ads, messaging, and even social content, with cohesive messaging, to avoid customers getting stuck at Level Three. Guiding your audience through a natural, simple, and intuitive journey is crucial at the bottom three levels. Once you know who you are talking to and what you are saying to them, you can fine-tune how you are communicating, to consistently ask the same thing of your audience with each touchpoint. You don't want to send someone to a landing page with multiple, competing CTAs (calls to action)! For now, you are still earning their trust, so distracting them is not the best idea.

It is so important at this level to know where your customer is coming from so that you are not serving them something that distracts them from your request. If your goal is to direct someone to your website, get them there quickly and ensure there are no further distractions once they're there. Don't make visitors wait while your website videos and images load; optimize your website so it loads quickly and has clear messaging. Avoid vague messages: have clear calls to action. If you want someone to buy a product, for example, don't have a pop-up that asks them to sign up for a newsletter.

The average time it takes to fully load the average mobile landing page is twenty-two seconds. However, research indicates 53 percent of people will leave a mobile page if it takes longer than three seconds to load.[4]

The same thinking applies to a brick-and-mortar store. Work on creating engagement and meaning with your storefront instead of chaos and distraction. Rachel Shechtman, the founder of Story (recently acquired by Macy's), is a friend of mine, who inadvertently used the Seventh Level Engagement Framework when developing her company. It was the attention to detail in providing a narrative-driven, engaging customer experience that led to Macy's acquisition of them to help with a retail issue.[5]

Story didn't know, but they applied the Seventh Level Engagement Framework to their branding by working with different companies to tell a story inside of their pop-up stores. The brands sponsored the story of a quarterly changing storefront in Chelsea. One quarter, the theme was women's empowerment and another quarter, it was STEM. The concept was to meld larger personal narratives and beliefs with meaning into a shoppable experience.

---

4   "Average Page Load Times for 2018—How Does Yours Compare?" *MachMetrics Speed Blog*, February 25, 2018, https://www.machmetrics.com/speed-blog/average-page-load-times-websites-2018/.

5   Lauren Sherman, "Macy's Acquires Story," *Business of Fashion*, May 2, 2018, https://www.businessoffashion.com/articles/bof-exclusive/macys-acquires-story and "Story: A Store to Explore inside Macy's," https://www.macys.com/social/story/.

You don't need the institutional backing of Macy's to pull this off; other companies can do the same. Storefronts are an opportunity to tell a meaningful story and connect with a customer—you just have to avoid showcasing products that take away from your messaging, aren't indicative of your larger offerings, and distract would-be customers from coming in.

In order for you to execute well in this level, it's key that you know your customer and the path you want them to embark on to reach your goal. Don't lose the opportunity to take your customer on a well-thought-out journey.

Ever find yourself falling asleep during a presentation? Chances are the deck has tons of words and very few visuals. These types of presentations don't speak to anyone and herein lies the importance of branding. When we designed a deck for Justin Baldoni's viral TED Talk, we made sure to work with him to keep things visually simple to understand with very little text. We do the same thing for every pitch deck we design for clients, as well as for my own presentations. Thoughtful, appropriate design, iconography, and visuals can help get your message across in a way that is easily digestible, which will help you combat frustrated engagement brought on by tedious, text-heavy slides whose content can't be jotted down in your notebook in time.

Or, perhaps, you've arrived on time to an invitation-only event to find the producers are *still* setting up the tables. They look frantic as they run over to register you. Your level of distraction is high in that moment. You aren't thinking about the purpose of the event itself, why you're there, or even about which speaker you're most excited to see. You're thinking about the noise of furniture moving around, whether or not you've arrived too early, or worst of all, what else have the organizers messed up?

When you plan an event, even the smallest ignored detail can prove catastrophically distracting. It is imperative that you take care of everything hours before your guests arrive—it seems obvious, but it's easier said than done. Make sure the wires are hidden from view, the linens are ironed, and the forks are all the same distance from the plates. As we like to say at CatalystCreativ, "You don't realize you're breathing air until it is polluted." Any experience you host should feel seamless to attendees, and taking care of details like timing or organized place settings helps tremendously to ensure your guests don't get stuck at Level Three.

ACTION, QUESTIONS, AND GOALS:
EXTERNAL CUSTOMERS

ACTION
An existing customer of the Online Mattress Company leaves the website without browsing other products after being served with a pop-up offering them a discount for a product they already purchased.

QUESTIONS
- Has the Online Mattress Company mapped out multiple customer journeys for various customer types?
- Do they understand what items people are likely to buy after they buy a mattress?
- Have they set up suitable triggers for various calls to action based on the data they have and/or actions actually taken by customers?

GOALS
- Email purchasers at the established intervals (thirty-, sixty-, and ninety-day check-in periods; six to twelve months) and offer ancillary purchase options, such as pillows and sheets.
- Email customers based on purchasing habits (i.e., they have to purchase X, so the next email offer is for Y).

- For those site visitors who the Online Mattress Company has previous session/purchase data for, customize the pop-up they are presented when visiting the site. For existing customers, present them with a pop-up discount offer on ancillary products (i.e., sheets, pillows, etc.). For new visitors, present them with a pop-up discount offer on a new mattress.
- For those site visitors who the Online Mattress Company does not have previous session/purchase data for, offer two pop-up options instead of one specific offer: one for those with a mattress and one for those without. The one the visitor selects will determine which offer they see—a discount to purchase a mattress or a discount to purchase ancillary products.

For Level Three, the Online Mattress Company's goal is to limit distractions when existing or new potential customers visit their website. They can do this by leveraging the technology they have to develop various pop-up user experiences on their website, that all serve to funnel visitors toward a desired outcome. They should ensure a site visitor isn't distracted by a message that is not relevant. Don't bombard people with a variety of requests in a variety of ways. Keep it simple and keep it consistent.

INTERNAL CUSTOMERS: IN THE WORKPLACE

There are several problems with frustrated engagement in the workplace. I like to use the example of our brand director. He has to do a lot of work that requires his full, undistracted attention. We are remote workers at Cata-lystCreativ, and we all share our calendars, so we can add appointments to each other's calendar. When our brand director has to work on something creative at a higher level of engagement, which could be Level Four for basic design work or Level Six for higher level, creative work (I'll discuss both levels in upcoming chapters), he blocks his calendar, snoozes almost all notifications, and asks that we do not send Slack messages or emails to him. If an emergency occurs, we can text him. He communicates what is best for him to limit distractions. As a leader, how often do we ask something of an employee, then Slack them with something else, then email them about yet another thing? We are constantly keeping our employ-ees at Level Three: Frustrated Engagement, when we should create boundaries with each other to ensure that workplaces are successful for each and every individual. We should also teach the people in our companies to set boundaries with colleagues and managers—even exec-utives—or nothing will ever get done! Whether you're in a busy office, working in a coffee shop, or spending the day working at home, there is a near-endless range of distractions that could tempt you to spend time away from what you're supposed to be working on.

Apps—particularly social media ones—have been designed to be deliberately addictive, rewarding our habits of "just checking" for notifications and to see if friends or celebrities have updated their profiles. The best way to prevent your smartphone tempting you during the workday is to turn it off or switch it to airplane mode. Although that might work for some people in certain fields, or if you're on a deadline, the reality is that turning off our phones completely is not a practical option for most of us—especially for those of us who use social media to advertise and engage with our customers. It's important, therefore, to set some rules for yourself to follow to limit your distractions. Perhaps you only check social media apps once a day, at 2 p.m., for example. Find what works for you so you don't fall down the rabbit hole of social media and waste a lot of your time.

The internet itself is also a huge distraction. Unfortunately, in working environments that are increasingly centered around online communications (whether through email or messaging apps) and browser-based systems, it can be difficult to disconnect and focus on other tasks.

Having conversations with coworkers is important for building a friendly, collaborative culture and atmosphere, but if left unchecked, spending too much time in conversation—or bad-natured gossip—is also hugely distracting. Be wary of your time sinks and work to minimize these and other distractions in the workplace so that you can work efficiently and effectively.

ACTION, QUESTIONS, AND GOALS:
INTERNAL CUSTOMERS

ACTION

Employees are interested in participating in a new goal-setting program and begin the task but are distracted by their daily duties and don't complete it.

QUESTIONS

- Have employees been given time for a goals working session, during which they can focus on goal-setting without distraction?
- Does the company display any follow-through on goal-setting?
- Has the leadership team shared the importance of setting goals and that the time spent will be respected by the rest of the company?
- Has the leadership team met with other department heads to prioritize the importance of goal-setting?
- Has leadership worked with each employee to block time on their calendars for goal-setting?
- Has the leadership team ensured they are not distracting employees during that time and asking more from them?

GOALS

- Set up a goals session to teach employees the value of goal-setting and how to set their goals.

- Find and share statistics of the impact goal-setting can have on personal/professional development and on company/department achievements.
- Build accountability and focused time with leadership by scheduling one-on-one sessions to discuss where each employee is on their path to setting their goals.
- Meet with other department heads to ensure they understand that their employees will need focused time between project deadlines for goal-setting.

For Level Three, the leadership team's goal is to find ways to clear the time and headspace for their employees to feel they can complete the task. They are working to limit the number of distractions to prevent their employees getting stuck at Level Three and not completing the goal-setting process. That means minimizing potentially redundant meetings and developing deeper understandings of what employees perceive as roadblocks to productivity in their days.

MOVING ON FROM PHASE 1 AND LEVEL THREE

Before you move to Phase 2 and Level Four, where you can ask someone for something, you have to ensure you have reached Levels One, Two, and Three, which are all about earning trust. To recap briefly before we move on to the second segment of the Seventh Level Engagement Framework, you've accomplished the following:

1. You know your audience.
2. You know how to properly speak to that audience.
3. You are limiting distractions and have created a proper customer journey for that audience.

Once you've learned about your audience, what they want, how they desire connection, and what's important to them, you can start to request action. Create the easiest path for engagement by limiting distractions so they move forward—whether that's generating a sale on your website or getting your employees to complete their tasks.

With a foundation of trust and understanding in place, the next two levels of the Seventh Level Engagement Framework involve more interaction. Because you know what matters to your audience, it's now okay to say, "I want you to do this for me."

PART THREE

PHASE 2: ENGAGE

Chapter Five

LEVEL FOUR: STRUCTURE-DEPENDENT ENGAGEMENT

IF IT'S SIMPLE, I'LL DO IT

Harry and Sally recover from the aforementioned ex-wife incident at Sharper Image and continue to develop their rapport and grow their friendship.

"I think you should wear skirts more," Harry says to Sally. "You look really good in skirts."

In a scene that closely follows, we see Sally as she's looking at a new apartment, wearing a skirt.

"You should get out there and date people," Sally says to Harry.

A few scenes later, he is out on a date with someone new.

Level Four is characterized by a person's active response to instruction, assuming the suggested action isn't too demanding. It shows a person is listening and receptive enough to consider your recommended action. As the movie continues, Sally and Harry start to trust one another more. They've connected through some unique experiences, and they've grown comfortable offering advice and suggestions to one another.

More importantly, they listen to each other's advice and suggestions.

I think of the first three levels as getting to know a person on a first date. By the time you've reached Level Four, you've been on a few dates and are ready to introduce them to your friends and your family. You're ready to invite them to work functions and participate in experiences that matter to you. A level of trust has been established, which means you've earned the right to ask something of them.

Welcome to Level Four: Structure-Dependent Engagement.

IF IT'S SIMPLE ENOUGH, I'LL DO IT

Structure-dependent engagement is instruction-based. There is little to no sacrifice on the part of the other person.

For example, Level Four engagement happens when all of the five-year-old students in a kindergarten classroom raise their hands after the teacher asks the students who are five to raise their hands. They are responding to the task; they are agreeing to participate. In marketing, this may look like a social media engagement, such as when you post an image that says, "Comment below with your favorite ice cream flavor," and people comment.

In this stage, people might find themselves saying, "If it's simple enough, I'll do it."

At this level, I am going to be talking a lot about social media engagement, despite that sort of engagement not necessarily being the ultimate, higher goal of a successful campaign. However, social media engagement—in the form of likes, comments, and accumulated followers—is for many people, synonymous with *meaningful* engagement, and this is especially true at Level Four. The problem with social media engagement at this level is that so many are settling for Level Four engagement. We've been told—and believe—engagement is having a certain number of followers who write comments on their feeds when asked. But we are not using the tools to determine our own version of success, we are letting them tell us what success looks like. This is more about the tools using us than us using the tools. Social media engagement measures the public's engagement by likes, shares, and comments. As I have mentioned, it is measuring the quantity of the "engagements" but what about the quality of response?

Have you ever eaten a bag of Cheez Doodles? (There's no shame in it! They're addictive!) At the bottom of the bag, once you're finished, all that's left is Cheez Doodle dust, the remnants of a once tasty snack. Viral hashtags are a lot like this Cheez Doodle dust. Instead of meaningful conversations with depth and intention, we get tiny vestiges of what was once a fully formed piece of "food." I'd like to see a rule that no one can share anything about anything until they read the entire article and cite their source. Imagine if the only way we could share about something is if we were actually informed! We retweet, comment, post, and like with a touch of a finger, and no real understanding of what we are digesting. We read half a headline and retweet it before we even know if it's real news.

Social media itself has become a popularity contest that you win by quantity, not quality. At its core, social media engagement is whenever someone interacts with your social media account.

It comes in the form of metrics such as:

- Likes
- Follows
- Shares
- Comments
- Retweets
- Click-throughs

Any way your audience interacts with you on platforms such as Twitter and Facebook is social media engagement. And these metrics are crucial for measuring the effectiveness of your social media campaign and accomplishing goals such as generating leads and sales. But they aren't nearly enough to build legitimate brand loyalty.

We need to own the conversation. We think Level Four is the highest level digitally, yet there are three more levels to go. We have more to offer our customers. Why aren't we setting our own engagement goals and then leveraging the tools we have—social media and otherwise—to help us get there?

Use your Seventh Level Statement as your guiding force so you aren't obsessed with vanity metrics like likes and followers for no reason. Set a higher reason for the work you are doing and how it fits into a larger narrative. One of the best examples of a brand that does this exceptionally well is Netflix. They have figured out a way to use their Seventh Level statement—which I would assess to be something like "entertainment should be personal"— as the lens through which they determine calls to action (CTAs) when asking their audience to comment on posts.

They aren't asking for comments just because. They are asking for comments to start a conversation with their audience, as well as between members of their audience. One of my favorite Level Four examples was a very simple Tweet: "Let's try something weird. Tell us the most bizarre thing you've overheard strangers say...and we'll give you a film recommendation for this weekend."

They used their Seventh Level Statement—entertainment should be personal—to create a Level Four call to action, and then they personally responded to the subsequent deluge of comments. With 104 comments and 2,400 likes, this effort was a success from a metrics standpoint, as well as from a deeper engagement one: fans of Netflix got to directly engage with the voice of the brand! This is the way you create a clear, concise ask, that people want to participate in, and that you can build off of. After all, not only did people respond to Netflix's question. There's a very good chance they went on to stream what the account recommended to them afterward.

Structure-dependent engagement happens when you

provide clear, concise instructions or requests to multiple people. It's a simple request, and it's something you know the people can accomplish—like asking everyone in the audience to raise their hand if they've seen *When Harry Met Sally...* In this example, you're getting participation, but at the least impactful level, and only because you asked explicitly for it.

IN EXTERNAL CUSTOMERS

You know you've reached Level Four if your customers react to your requests via your communication channels. Remember, you can't get to Level Four without ensuring Levels One, Two, and Three are met. For you to assess where your audience is and understand how to get them to higher levels of engagement, you have to not only earn their trust but also maintain that trust.

When you host an event and want your audience to do something, such as listen to a presentation, make sure that the microphone works (Level One), that the speaker uses terminology the audience will understand (Level Two), and that atmospheric distractions are limited (Level Three) so that the ask is clear and concise and easy to act on (Level Four).

If you have someone onstage asking for people to participate or listen or raise their hand or dance, then make sure the bar isn't open. Use the physical experience to direct the audience. If you want people to be quiet, make sure the lights are dim, and then put the spotlight on the stage and ask people to be quiet. If you want people's attention, create an experience that has a clear call to action and limit distractions while you are doing so—remember Levels One, Two, and Three. At Level Four, make the asks simple and easy to digest, and frame them by using the experience to enhance the calls to action, not take away from them.

It's crucial to recognize the importance of branding at Level Four. Suppose you launch a campaign on social media that asks people to do something, like comment on several posts. But every post is of a random visual of a person swimming, while you ask your audience to comment with the name of their favorite sneaker. Your brand strategy needs to be consistent with what you represent and also consistently applied to all communications. Make sure you create simple graphics that state your message and clearly communicate your Seventh Level Statement and a concise call to action. More and more brands are using Instagram as a visual gallery of their experiences. Take Death Wish Coffee's Instagram, for instance. They have a visual appeal with clear calls to actions, using branding as a mechanism to get people to respond to Level Four prompts.[6] Match your

6   Death Wish Coffee, Instagram, https://www.instagram.com/deathwishcoffee/?hl=en.

visuals with your relevant calls to action and keep posts on-brand to minimize barriers to your audience taking the desired action.

The truth is, you're probably already doing most of these things most of the time, but you're not experiencing the success you want because you're not doing them in a cohesive way. Continue to think about the lower levels as you maintain and build relationships. Even though audience members' engagement may be fluctuating (which is normal), you want to have efforts in place that are constantly propelling them toward reaching the Seventh Level.

Depending on the size of your audience, to maintain trust with subgroups who might have shifted to lower than desired levels, you might need to segment out your efforts. Segmentation allows you to customize how you communicate with each group. It's not always easy to accomplish, but tending to backsliding groups proactively is easier and more cost-effective than starting from scratch.

If you do not think about Levels One, Two, and Three while you are tending to audiences who are already in the highest levels, you will, by default, drop your customers back to lower levels. It takes way more time, effort, and money to go back and start again than it does to maintain. You might think someone who's engaged will stay engaged, but you have to do the sticky work. The good news is, once you get someone to Level Four, it's not as difficult to keep them there by keeping them engaged.

Examples include asking your customers to comment on a post, follow you on social media, retweet a tweet, or sign up to an email list. These very simple instruction-based asks build your relationship with your customer while you're still getting to know them and they're getting to know you. You might ask them to like an image, and they like it. You might ask them to answer a poll, and they answer all the questions. You might ask them to share one of your posts, and they do so. Your customers aren't necessarily doing anything of their own volition, but they are willing to do what you've asked because it's easy and doesn't require too much effort.

Companies often get stuck in Level Four with their customers because it's easy and provides measurable marketing data, although not the most meaningful data. You repeatedly ask for simple tasks, your customers oblige, and then it's over. As mentioned earlier, most people think of Level Four as the definition of engagement, and so we are settling for a lower level of engagement. Stopping here doesn't lead to sustainable, meaningful relationships with our customers or employees. We think we reached the summit at Level Four, but we really are just at base camp, and there are still three more levels to scale.

Your customers don't want to stay at this level forever. They will eventually stop engaging and fulfilling your low-level requests if the engagement stops there. That's why it's important to follow up and bring your audience to the next level (which we'll discuss in the next chapter).

ACTIONS, QUESTIONS, GOALS: EXTERNAL CUSTOMERS

ACTION

The Online Mattress Company's Instagram followers will comment on the company's posts when they're prompted directly in the caption.

QUESTIONS

- Is the company using the lens of their Seventh Level Statement to determine what calls to action or social media strategy they are using to elicit comments?
- Are they posting questions with content that is truly of interest to their followers' values and beliefs?
- Has the company looked at competitors and the types of calls to action they are using to engage their followers?
- Has the company analyzed the types of calls to action that have been most successful in eliciting comments in the past?

- Have they been encouraging and responding to the few followers who have shared or commented on their content?

GOALS

- Assign a community manager to monitor and respond to and/or like all post comments.
- Follow up individually with those who share via post as well as direct messages, when appropriate.
- Read comments and show gratitude publicly for followers who have commented in the desired, appropriate way, highlighting conversations that align with the company's Seventh Level Statement.

At this level, the Online Mattress Company's goal is to engage with its audience by asking them to take a small, desired action, then acknowledging that participation in an authentic way. This request should be reasonable and simple for their followers and should contribute to improving the metrics the company is aiming to improve. By the Online Mattress Company showing appreciation for those who comment, they can maintain audience engagement and open the door for future, higher-level engagement as well—this can be something as simple as responding to a comment.

INTERNAL CUSTOMERS: IN THE WORKPLACE

In the workplace, the Level Four engagement is common among low- and midlevel employees who clock in, complete the tasks that they've been given, and then clock out. They show up and check off their to-do lists, but they're not necessarily coming up with the ideas on their own; they're merely executing them. Without constant hand-holding or constant managing, they would just sit there twiddling their thumbs. They lack initiative.

The tasks are basic and offer safety, ease, and comfort to the employees. They can follow through with the task, they understand what is being asked of them, and they were spoken to in the correct manner. "Sure, I'll do that."

Based on an analysis of the current workplace and many conversations with baby boomers, such as my father, it seems as if up to the time of the internet, a job was a job for most employees. People weren't looking for meaning and identity in the workplace; they came to work, did their tasks, and went home to connect with family and friends. Work stayed at work. Today, the line between work and home has blurred. The internet allows us to work anywhere, anytime, all the time—for better or worse. We identify with our work and want a job that has value and aligns with who we are. Millennials, Gen Zers, the millennial-minded, and humans in general are looking for more from workplaces. As employers, we still need to earn their trust in Levels One, Two, and Three. And Level Four is still important—a lot of work is doing what you are asked. People need to work for reasons beyond fun and purpose, so these first four levels are still highly relevant to successful workplaces.

In my own company, we have multiple generations represented. My dad, who handles business strategy and development for us, comes from a generation where Level Four employees were the norm. His experience was critical for me as I strived to reach Seventh Level engagement while maintaining Level Four. We can't reach the higher levels without the midlevels.

We're limited on our current understanding of engagement. People need to know what they're doing and have responsibilities and do what they're supposed to be doing. Level Four is what workplace engagement traditionally looked like—do this, do that. Obviously, we need Level Four engagement for work to happen, but the workplace needs to change to enable the higher levels. People are looking for freedom, flexibility, and a place where they can learn who they are and grow. Level Four is limiting in this regard.

Later in the book, I will be talking about the way I have set up my company as a self-organized structure instead of a traditional hierarchy. I personally did not want to have a company where I had to hold people's hands to get the job done. I hired the people I hired because they are better at what they do than I am—why else would I need to hire them in the first place?

Throughout the years, employees' desires and demands have evolved, and it can be challenging for companies to keep up. Employers are bombarded with a wide range of trendy tips for keeping different generations of workers happy. When it comes to attracting and retaining top talent, employers need to understand what employees really want from a company. While we all know that competitive pay and good benefits factor (Level Five, more on that very soon) into an employee's decision to join and stay at a company, there are many other overlooked desires that can be as important as a paycheck.

To truly enjoy their jobs, employees must feel that their employers respect them and will provide them with what they need to be successful in both their professional and personal lives. The 2018 Global Talent Trends study by Mercer[7] revealed a few employee desires that many organizations seem to be missing.

The study took a multiperspective approach and collected input from 800 business executives and 1,800 HR leaders, as well as more than 5,000 employees across 21 industries and 44 countries around the world. Mercer gathered these voices to analyze how both employers and employees are reimagining the future of work. The study identified top talent trends, which can be useful

7   "Connectivity in the Human Age: Global Talent Trends 2019," Mercer Global, https://www.mercer.com/our-thinking/career/global-talent-hr-trends.html.

for companies who are trying to stay ahead of the game when it comes to employee satisfaction.

Among the findings, Mercer identified three factors that employees and job candidates are looking for in a company: permanent workplace flexibility, a commitment to health and well-being, and working with a purpose.

Based on my thesis, I learned that with higher engagement comes higher productivity, so why are we settling for Level Four?

ACTION, QUESTIONS, GOALS: INTERNAL CUSTOMERS

ACTION

When asked, employees take an HR survey that requires less than two minutes to complete.

QUESTIONS

- How is the company showing the employees that they are listening to the survey responses?
- Is the company replying to each employee, thanking them for their time?
- How did the company develop the questions? Does the intention of the survey align with the company's Seventh Level Statement?

GOALS

- Share the survey responses with employees to showcase what is important to the organization and how the company is taking action on their results.
- Contact each employee who participated using their preferred communication method to thank them for their time.
- Create a postsurvey plan of action and share it with employees to let them know how their answers will be used and that their time is valued.

At Level Four, the company's goal is to acknowledge employees who have completed the desired action and thank them for it. Showing appreciation for those who do what's requested is a simple way to maintain employee engagement and open the door for future, higher-level engagement as well. It should go without saying, but a simple thank-you email in these cases can go a long way!

MOVING ON FROM LEVEL FOUR

Level Four encourages simple engagement or interaction. At this level, engaging with your customer has become a two-way street; since you have already earned your customer's trust through the work you put in at Levels One through Three, you can ask them to complete a simple task, and they'll likely complete it. You don't have your audience where you want them yet, but this is a start and a jumping off point for the higher levels of engagement you and your customers—internal and external—ultimately crave.

At Level Four, your audience is doing what you're asking of them because the request is small and requires next to no sacrifice on their part. You say, "Jump," and before they decide, they ask, "How high?" Assuming your response is, "Oh, don't worry about jumping *too* high, whatever you feel comfortable with," they'll do it!

But a company built solely on employees complying with simple requests has a pretty low ceiling. Micromanaging all of your employees gets exhausting and won't lead to any new or innovative ideas. Similarly, a marketing campaign with the ultimate goal of getting a bunch of likes on a few social posts really won't move the needle in terms of a brand's bottom line, especially if you have no strategy on why you are asking for likes in the first place.

The thing is, because at Level Four you are seeing *some* sort of result, it's easy and quite common for companies to get stuck here. Maybe you're at Level Four right now yourself! You see your internal customers/employees doing the work you told them to do, but to what end? You find yourself having to ask for every single task to be completed, which is starting to become a bit of a time suck.

Or maybe you see your audience liking and commenting on a ton of your posts, or opening your emails, but you're struggling to get anyone to do anything more than a simple request of liking or commenting. It feels impossible to get customers to share anything you post or fill out a survey. You're asking them to jump a little bit higher, but to no avail. As you continue to build the relationship with your audience, you will end up finding that starting with Level Four is a good way to interact with and maintain the relationship with your customers, but if you want to keep asking them to do something, you will want to offer something in return, which ends up being the next step up from Level Four.

You have done so much work to get your audience to this point, but they are still doing the bare minimum of what you are asking for and not anything more. That's because what you are requesting of them in a more meaningful way requires more of them, but you aren't giving anymore of yourself to them in return.

To get someone to take the time to give you more of their time and energy, you better be prepared to offer something that is valuable to them. This is Level Five—where your customers are asking, "What can you do for me?"

Moving on to Level Five successfully is all about the offer and what you are doing to pique someone's excitement— the carrot on the stick. It's crucial at every level to ensure that you are operating from a place of authenticity and connecting with your audience with what makes the most sense for you and for them. At Level Five, that means ensuring that what you are offering is aligned with what you are asking, for both you and your audience.

You wouldn't want to give away a free car if you weren't getting something valuable in return. You also wouldn't want to give away a free car if it had nothing to do with what your campaign was about or what your brand represents, or what your audience cares about. You need to evaluate whether what you are offering—or how you are offering it—is enough, and that what you are asking for is valuable for you.

That's why influencer and microinfluencer marketing, sweepstakes, integrated brand partnerships, free events, bonus pools, commission structures, free snacks, and Ping-Pong tables can prove helpful at Level Five. The carrot on the stick garners excitement from your audience just enough to keep engaging with you.

Chapter Six

LEVEL FIVE: SELF-REGULATED INTEREST

WHAT'S IN IT FOR ME?

While at the batting cage with his friend, Harry is asked why he spends so much time with Sally. Perhaps out of machismo, Harry boasts that he's getting something out of his still-platonic relationship with Sally—namely, that he gets a woman's perspective on things.

Harry enjoys Sally's company because of what's in it for him.

Many people keep a relationship afloat because of what's in it for them and how it makes their lives easier. Harry isn't the only one getting something out of the friendship. Sally wants Harry around to help her take care of things in her own life too. For instance, she uses Harry to help her around the house in repositioning a rug.

Level Five is characterized by excitement, but the engagement is driven by self-interest rather than an interest in another individual or organization. Harry and Sally are both in it for partially selfish reasons. They aren't necessarily using each other, but there's not a lot of sacrifice for one another either. They don't have to give much other than serving some of the needs of the other person, and those aren't even emotional needs.

Level Five is like airline points; you stick with a carrier because you've accumulated their points, and switching means losing them. You see Level Five engagement a lot with workers—they don't love their job, but the money and benefits keep them around.

BUT WHAT'S IN IT FOR ME?

Level Five involves piquing someone's interest and fostering their self-excitement. They are interested because the engagement serves them in some way. Level Five is an easy place to land in terms of engagement for most people. "What's in it for me?" is a place most people operate throughout their entire lives.

Picture a student who plays on the basketball team but hates math. His teacher offers him extra credit for participating in class by answering a question each day. He's not going to class because he likes math and is hoping to learn more; rather, it piques his interest because he wants a good grade, which keeps him eligible to play on the basketball team. Extra credit is an example of Level Five engagement.

Level Five in marketing often entails a sweepstakes, discount, referral code, or other incentive that entices customers to do something because they get something. This can be especially effective when partnered with a celebrity or influencer—so it's a more relatable presence offering up a referral code or encouraging participation on behalf of your brand.

For companies, the "What's in it for me?" can play to both sides. Many businesses don't want to provide discounts on their products. They don't believe in incentives because they worry the customer will want more, more, more! But then, the company is really thinking about themselves too. They want to retain money and please stakeholders. The key is to begin thinking, "What's going to pique my customers' interest?" It's a combination of considering the company's message and goals while at the same time considering the customers' needs and wants.

Yes, Level Five is about incentives, but don't let yourself

get too carried away with the notion that your audience wanting something from you is a bad thing. Part of the idea behind Level Five is, before this, your audience probably wouldn't have been taking specific and meaningful actions with your brand. The incentive catalyzes them to cross that threshold and move into the next level of engagement with you.

At Level Five, you can easily drop down to a lower level of engagement if you don't have a strategy to build a more meaningful relationship based on the incentive. The incentive isn't sticky, and when done carelessly, can cause distraction. So you've got to think about what actions you want your audience to take past the point of incentive.

The old workplace paradigm in terms of engagement is generally Level Four. Employees need their basic needs met—we've all read about Maslow's hierarchy of needs. At Level Four, employees do only what is asked of them because they want to make sure they are making the right amount of money and getting their vacation days and 401(k) contributions. At Level Five, self-regulated interest can look like giving employees comp days for working overtime—anything that incentivizes going above and beyond the bare minimum. While that is important, we are still not at the highest levels of engagement. It is crucial at this level to note that Level Five is not the end-all, be-all of engagement.

Daniel Pink talks about this in his TED Talk. Financial incentives do not spur creativity, so at this level, it is important to remember that while you can certainly use these incentives to hire a person or incite productivity, you can't necessarily use them to inspire someone—more on that later when talking about Level Six.

Self-regulated interest, as the name implies, involves self-interest and excitement about what they'll get. This level centers around "What's in it for me?" That isn't necessarily a bad thing; however, it's hard to build a company or relationship that's based on incentives. It's a two-way street, but it's not genuine—they're doing something to get something—and eventually the incentives lose their excitement. How do you build the bridge between the incentive and their personal values and beliefs?

IN EXTERNAL CUSTOMERS

At this stage, you're still having to offer something for someone to connect with you.

Incentives can lead to a lot of falloff because companies don't know how to build off of them. They use these carrots on sticks without knowing the full customer journey and how they can leverage it to tell a bigger story through the lens of their Seventh Level. The Seventh Level Engagement Framework is centered around a user journey, so the carrot has to contribute to your customer's journey. How are you creating a map for your user to go from a passive consumer (Level One) to an active participant (the Seventh Level) with your brand?

Use your Seventh Level Statement as a lens when identifying what carrots to offer, celebrities to work with, partners to work with. Don't simply choose a random celeb that has a large following. Make sure the sentiment of those followers and what that celebrity's brand stands for matches what you stand for.

That's why I had you begin with your own Seventh Level Statement at the beginning of the book. Your Seventh Level Statement allows you to stay authentic throughout the whole framework. When you create a social media strategy at Level Four, you are using your Seventh Level as the lens in which you communicate. At Level Five, when you determine influencers and partners to work with, you are using your Seventh Level Statement to communicate *why* you chose what you chose as an incentive/partnership. Only then does it feel authentic and genuine to your customers. At Level Five, you're still asking someone to do something, and if they don't do what you ask, you tend to want to offer a carrot. The carrot is self-regulated interest and incentive.

For a lot of brands, marketing at this level centers a lot on influencer partnerships. Brands look for an influencer—a celebrity, for example—to partner with so that the company's products or services reach the influencer's following. It doesn't always have to be a celebrity either. We have worked with a lot of companies who are also interested in partnering with what we call in marketing "microinfluencers" or influencers, or other[8] brands that connect with their demographic. You see these partnerships a lot in the beauty industry, the health and wellness industry, and with brands involved in the family lifestyle market. If a company wants to market a new juice box for kids, for example, they search for mom bloggers and influencers who have a strong following to partner with.

The influencer marketing industry is booming at the moment. Companies are paying thousands, if not millions, of dollars to influencers to share products with their followers. The problem with that is the focus needs to be about deep engagement, not the idea of choosing someone because they have a lot of followers. With self-regulated interest, there can be a drop-off if a company isn't thoughtful about how to connect followers to their brand in a deep and meaningful way, which is why it's crucial to always be thinking about the lower levels as you go higher—don't build a house on sand; have a strong

8   Dan Boylan, "Census Bureau's First-Ever Online Headcount Designed to Reach Millennials Likely to Miss Mark," *The Washington Times*, March 14, 2019.

foundation in which you build from—and think about your Seventh Level Statement.

Thinking about who to work with for a product to market takes a lot of time, energy, and effort. You want to ensure your partnership aligns with your Seventh Level Statement and that you create context for why you are choosing such a partner. Celebrity endorsements can be tricky and can backfire easily.

For example, when being interviewed for an article in the *Washington Post*, I was told by the journalist that the Census Bureau was thinking about reaching out to partner with LeBron James because he could connect with younger residents who typically don't complete census forms. I know if I saw that ad, I would think, what the heck does LeBron James have to do with the Census Bureau? Without context, most people will make up their own reason, along the lines of "How much is this person really getting paid, or what's in it for them?" We are so used to being marketed to by influencers or microinfluencers that if it doesn't feel authentic, we will not trust the brand anymore. Poor partnering becomes a distraction, and rather than increase our engagement levels, we fall to lower levels of engagement.

When thinking about an influencer, it is not just about how many followers or how many likes or comments they get but who is following them and what they are saying. Analyze the sentiment behind the comments, not just the number of comments.

When thinking about a celebrity for a new baby brand that is being released, my company reviewed multiple celebrities and reviewed what people said in the comments. We ended up choosing an influencer that had meaningful comments related to parenthood as a conversation in his social media, not just thousands and thousands of comments saying, "You look hot in that outfit." Quantity does not equal quality. Brands falter when they identify a celebrity instead of creating a thoughtful campaign that includes a celebrity as one part of the strategy. If you don't give the why behind your choice, millennials and Gen Zers will write you off as a "SnapTimer."

Marketers need to choose influencers based on how we are teaching you to define engagement, not how the social media tools define engagement. Comments are changing; they're becoming a place to connect with others like chat rooms or campfires, mimicking our same human behaviors as before. In an article in *The Atlantic* titled, "How Comments Became the Best Part of Instagram,"[9] Taylor Lorenz writes, "The comment section is

---

9   Taylor Lorenz, "How Comments Became the Best Part of Instagram," *The Atlantic*, January 4, 2019. https://www.theatlantic.com/technology/archive/2019/01/how-comments-became-best-part-instagram/579415/.

increasingly where connections are made...Comments by Celebs's other co-founder, Julie Kramer, said 'Instagram's comment section acts as a natural watering hole for people with shared interests.'" Why do others follow that person specifically? What is in it for them? And then once the company identifies key influencers, it's important to determine how to communicate the details of your product in a meaningful and authentic way to their audience. Once the company has the attention of the influencer's followers, they then need to create context for them so that they can convert them to that next level.

Take the idea of an influencer who is a yoga instructor partnering with a supplement company. Their posts are mostly photos of them doing yoga poses in front of scenic backdrops. Then suddenly they post a photo of a health and wellness supplement. Their followers might feel taken aback and a little frustrated, as it feels inauthentic. The brand has to be more creative in the way the message is related. The brand partner could start by asking the yoga influencer, "What are the five major things that your network follows you for?" Using those answers, maybe the brand creates an experience—a free class, a free tip, or a way to communicate with this influencer. For the content itself, perhaps organize a photoshoot of the instructor doing their typical yoga poses but with the supplement incorporated into the shots in creative ways. The caption should be in the influencer's voice, be upfront about the partnership, and explain why the brand and personality align. It's important as well for the influencer to be informed on the product they are promoting on the brand's behalf so they can answer questions their fans might have, intelligently and authentically. Most recently, Seed, known for their probiotic supplements, devised a program called Seed University,[10] which required their affiliates or influencers to pass an exam before endorsing their products. It might seem like an extra step at first glance, but cementing this degree of accountability between brands and their partners can go a long way toward building a partnership's authenticity and viability.

We have worked with many brands who have chosen to approach microinfluencers over traditional celebrities. These microinfluencers have generally fewer than ten thousand followers, but these followers are perfect from a targeting standpoint. Their audience generally follows them for a very specific reason, such as their expertise in a field or because they engage with their audiences on a more regular basis.

As a marketer, a thought-out strategy is key. It's not enough that an influencer has a lot of followers. Know your intended audience and look for influencers whose

---

10 Anne Quito, "A New 'University' for Instagram Influencers Aims to Stop the Spread of Misinformation," *Quartzy*, July 23, 2019. https://qz.com/quartzy/1666740/seed-launches-a-university-for-instagram-influencers/.

Seventh Level Statement approximates your own. Make sure you know why the influencer's audience follows them and that their followers' reasons align with why you want them to engage with you. Be choosy with the influencers you work with and even choosier with the way that you work with those influencers.

If I were to look at an influencer program, I would choose to work with three major influencers over the course of a year—not thirty influencers (who tend to cost a lot of money). I would suggest building a meaningful relationship with these influencers and create a user experience that is authentic. Develop a program for engagement. Create a video or conduct a photoshoot that demonstrates the alignment between you and the influencer. Too many people—especially millennials and Gen Zers—see right through the inauthentic posts. The message from the influencer has to match the integrity of the organization; otherwise, you might disappoint your fans.

Sweepstakes are also a key strategy for Level Five, but they have to mean something. Work with strategic partners and develop a way to share your message through a sweepstakes campaign. Create a story behind the sweepstakes that communicates your brand.

Ogilvy, a renowned, international marketing agency produced a thoughtful, social media campaign[11] for Hellman's mayonnaise that aligned with Hellman's values while incentivizing customers to participate. In *The Restaurant with No Food* Hellman's asked people to post their leftovers on social media to enter a contest to win dinner prepared by a celebrity chef. Winners then brought their leftovers to a restaurant where celebrity chefs used them to create a five-star meal. Instead of the bill, customers received the recipe for their meal, and Hellman's posted a video of each recipe on their social channels. The message was that we shouldn't waste food, which is a value that Hellman's and their customers share. Even customers who didn't win the grand prize could see the recipes and videos about what to do with leftovers. They learned something and began to think differently about food. This campaign got others to think about themselves differently and inspired others to set goals. Hellman's did Levels One through Five (understanding their audience, making a simple request, free dinner, celebrity chefs, offerings and incentives) with the intention of Level Six (inspiring others to think about food differently) and the Seventh Level in the process (They aligned people's values and beliefs with what Hellman's stands for: they communicate that "we care about sustainability" first and foremost on their About section of their website.[12]) It was a perfect campaign.

---

11   Olgilvy, "The Restaurant with No Food," LinkedIn, https://www.linkedin.com/feed/update/urn:li:ugcPost:6534860428613300224.

12   Hellman's, "We Care about Sustainability," https://www.hellmanns.com/us/en/we-care-about-sustainably-sourced-ingredients.html.

It's critical to first determine what you stand for and what you believe in (your Seventh Level Statement), then utilize that to help you inform the partners, celebrities, and influencers you should be working with.

ACTION, QUESTIONS, GOALS: EXTERNAL CUSTOMERS

ACTION

The Online Mattress Company partners with a celebrity influencer to launch a sweepstakes wherein their audience can enter to win a chance to have that celebrity deliver a new mattress to their house. To enter, the audience must share their personal answer to "what they're driven to do every day—on a good night's sleep" on Instagram.

QUESTIONS

- Have they gathered enough information to confirm that this is an incentive that would be effective with their target audience?
- Is the celebrity influencer promotion connecting with the self-interest of their customers?
- Does this celebrity align with their brand values and beliefs (i.e., their Seventh Level Statement)?

- Are the incentive and incentivized behavior of commiserate value? (i.e., Is what's being offered by the company enough for the customer to take action? Is the desired customer action appropriately valuable for the incentive offered?)

GOALS

- Do appropriate research and informal surveying to identify the right celebrity influencer to capture the interest of their target audience.
- Conduct in-depth analysis of what the top five topics this celebrity influencer stands for.
- Analyze the behavior of the celebrity's social media followers beyond just the size of their audience.
- Ensure that the celebrity influencer is authentically connected to the brand and willing to provide a mutually beneficial messaging and promotional strategy (not just "pay to post").

The Online Mattress Company's goal is to identify what type of incentive this target audience would find most appealing. Level Five is all about "What's in it for me" and strategically providing an incentive to customers that is authentically aligned with your brand and that of the celebrity/microinfluencer partner.

INTERNAL CUSTOMERS: IN THE WORKPLACE

In the workplace at Level Four, employees are doing things because it's part of their job. At Level Five, they do more but need to be incentivized to do so.

Levels Four and Five are the status quo of workplaces. Employees get their work done, but it's not from a place of delighting the customer or growing the company. For older generations, work was nearly exclusively transactional: "Do what I ask of you, and you will get paid." Level Five was the highest an employer could expect an employee to reach. But because people are now looking for more transparency from work, incentives can only go so far, and the carrot on the stick might not be enough to bring employees to a place of deeper conversation. Eventually, for higher engagement, you have to understand the needs of your employees, and your employees have to understand the company's needs too.

I understand and acknowledge the personal importance of someone coming to me and asking for a raise. I have no problem with an employee doing what's best for them. Higher levels of engagement require piquing an employee's interest and paying them the value they deserve. When someone comes to me, presents their value, how they benefit the company, and asks for a raise, I consider their request seriously. The problem arises when someone asks for a raise just because they need or want it without identifying the company's needs or wants.

It is a natural thing for human beings to think about themselves first. We all need our needs met. There's nothing wrong with making sure you have what you need to feel happy. However, at this transactional level it's important to think about the other side of the equation of what you can provide in return for getting what you want. What's the ask and what's the offer and are they equal, whether it's a raise or an employer's request? Employers have to think of it as a two-way street.

As an employee, I would show my value to the company, then reach out to my boss, and ask for an appropriate raise.

Oftentimes, it's not even about the money. The key at this level of engagement is to find out what drives or motivates your employees to do their job well and engage with the company. I once had an employee who wanted to change careers from marketing to events. She didn't have the professional background to make this change, but she wanted to make more money and try out a new career. We shifted her position from marketing, where she was neither happy nor doing her best work, to events, where she prospered and grew. We were able to eventually pay her more because she excelled at doing work she wanted to do that also fulfilled a company need.

Another employee wanted to get her PhD. She asked if she could shift to part time for a year and then transition out of the company. We turned a situation that could have been just self-serving for the employee and made it work for both parties. She was able to approach us with the idea because our company has a culture that is open and supportive. She thought about possible solutions and came up with the one that wouldn't leave us high and dry.

ACTION, QUESTIONS, GOALS: INTERNAL CUSTOMERS

ACTION
A company rolls out a monetary incentive program for employees to reach their goals.

QUESTIONS
- Is this the right incentive to capture the employees' interest?
- Does this incentive align with their brand values and beliefs (i.e., their Seventh Level Statement)?
- Do employees see the value beyond the incentive?
- How will this incentive aid in continued quality of productivity?

GOALS
- Survey employees to ask what they value most (i.e., paid time off, coffee, lunch, classes, books).

- Get the leadership, employees, and other stakeholders behind the larger company mission that this program works toward achieving.
- Establish clear guidelines around how goals should be aligned with workloads in order to balance the employee's desire to achieve and their desire to win the incentive.
- Find and implement additional options for incentivizing employees that are value-based, rather than financial.

At this level, the company should carefully consider potential incentives before selecting one to offer to employees in return for them meeting their individual goals. It's important to be sure that the value of the incentive is commensurate with the value of what it will produce for the company. Level Four requests can increase interaction, but maintaining or growing that connection generally requires Level Five engagement in the form of this sort of incentive. For optimum impact, the incentive should align with the brand and the brand's employees' personal values and beliefs.

CLIMBING HIGHER

Sometimes people will do what you ask of them because it is a low barrier to entry, but sometimes you want to ask more from them, and that requires a bit of an incentive. Because engagement is a two-way street, it's your turn again to engage again. Following up after your audience has completed your initial task ushers them into Level

Five. Level Five is transactional; it goes beyond positive reinforcement. At Level Five, people begin to ask, "What's in it for me?"

Working with microinfluencers is key at Level Five. Since you are likely now asking more of your audience, microinfluencers—online personalities your audience already feels connected to at an intimate level—can help humanize and soften your request. These accounts have real relationships with people who might in turn spread your product and message. This creates an experience that builds off people's true networks.

Make sure you're creating the proper user journey. Send personalized emails that identify this partnership as intentional. "Hey, we see that you love this influencer's Instagram account, and they suggested we reach out because this is what we have in common!" Lay out how and why this partnership makes sense from a brand ethos standpoint. At Level Five it's essential to use branding as a way to build a narrative and integrate microinfluencers and influencers into a comprehensive experience that represents both you and their brands. Bumble created beautiful branded visuals for their campaign with microinfluencers and influencers. Their branding was clear and concise, and geared toward NYC residents, featuring NYC influencers. The branding enhanced the experience for both the influencers and the audience. Influencers were proud to participate, and it felt like an authentic connection for both the brand and the participants; it piqued the excitement of the influencers because they were offered to be featured in a beautiful, branded campaign.

Often in sales and marketing or as bosses, we think that our customers and our employees have to do what we want without us giving them a reason to. In reality, we have to build a foundation of trust so that we don't have to constantly ask them to do something. They actually just want to do it. Incentivizing going above and beyond is a crucial step.

Level Five also plays a big role in charity events. A nonprofit is looking to fundraise and ask for your money, and while giving to nonprofits helps you feel warm and fuzzy inside and hopefully moves you to Level Six through a deeper connection with a cause, there are so many different charities to choose from! It is important that nonprofits have some type of Level Five incentive to get you to say yes initially. The many gala events we have produced included a major performer or a spokesperson, gift bags, and other incentives that get someone to attend, because deep down even though it is always about the charity, people are still giving their time or money to participate in an experience and want to know what's in it for them. Whatever the perk, we're certain the values associated with it align with the values of the organization it's helping promote.

By this point you've been very thoughtful about who you're partnering with, what you're using for an incentive, and how you're connecting. Now it's time to think about how you connect meaningfully and build off that relationship by taking it from transactional to inspirational, and emotionally supportive. To use an easy-to-understand metaphor, this is the phase where you go from "going steady" to getting married.

The highest two levels focus on the highest terms of engagement: delighting others.

You're finally at a point in the framework where you won't just settle for a transactional exchange. You now want to build loyalty and have a meaningful relationship. These levels are important because they meet the needs of the person. You're someone they think will make their life better—whether it's a partner, a client, or an employee. You are moving them past the "What's in it for me?" into "How can I become the best version of me for the relationship?"

People will begin to evolve and change because your messaging reflects your Seventh Level Statement, which aligns with theirs. They will start to feel like their best selves and connect with you more deeply and meaningfully. This requires that you have a company worth believing in. We can no longer settle for an isolated corporate social responsibility. If you have a marketing campaign or commercial on gender equality, you will look pretty foolish if your new followers start investigating and find out you have a board full of only men.

Walk the walk! Everyone has access to company information nowadays. Be careful where you donate your money. Treat your employees and contractors fairly. Be cognizant of where you source materials. You need to be able to defend every one of your actions or you will never reach the Seventh Level of engagement.

The final two levels are where customers and employees are obsessed with your product. They are passionate, inspired, and ignited by your brand. Welcome to Phase 3!

PART FOUR

PHASE 3: DELIGHT

Chapter Seven

LEVEL SIX: CRITICAL ENGAGEMENT

I'M INSPIRED

As their friendship develops further, Harry and Sally begin to challenge each other and legitimately force one another to grow as individuals. In one scene, Harry and Sally get into a fight outside their friends' home after they helped move in a wagon wheel coffee table. Harry calls Sally out for never getting upset over an ex leaving her.

"Nothing bothers you," Harry tells her. "You never get upset about anything."

Sally gets angry and strikes back.

"You're going to have to move back to New Jersey because you slept with everyone in New York."

They apologize, but the result of the conversation is that both characters change and are inspired by what the other person said. In one of the next scenes, Sally calls Harry hysterically crying because her ex-husband got married.

"I need a tissue!" Sally tells Harry.

She shows that she's willing to be vulnerable. Meanwhile, Harry gets into a relationship and starts to settle down. They trust one another and their opinions and are willing to risk making changes.

Level Six is characterized by a person feeling inspired enough to set goals to make a change in their own life.

I'M INSPIRED TO CHANGE

Critical engagement is a moment of enlightenment. It's a level where someone is inspired and catalyzed to set goals to transform themselves. They want to grow and change as an individual or organization.

Imagine a first grader who learns that sea turtles are affected by plastic in the ocean and then sets goals to recycle for the rest of his life.

Think about your favorite brands and the way they make you think about your own life. I am a huge Disney World fan and have been going since I was a child. And to this day, every time I see that Disney logo or a Disney store or a Disney movie, I'm reminded of how this brand has helped me set goals to change the way I think about experiences in my own life. I invest in experiences that inspire and educate that make people feel differently about themselves because of Disney. If associated with a powerful enough brand, even a logo can impact behavioral change!

While the famed recycling logo might not be a "brand" in the conventional sense, it's an almost universally recognizable image that elicits a desired response. When you are holding an empty soda can and you see a bin with the recycling logo, you instinctively recycle it because you're inspired to. In doing so, you are helping a cause/brand (eliminating waste in an environmentally conscious way) and feeling good about contributing in a small way. That's Critical Engagement.

An event is a good example of a time when inspiration plays a big role in changing the way people think about their behavior. We worked with a client called Biossance to launch their brand in Canada and wanted to create an experience that communicated their beliefs in No Compromise Beauty. Biossance avoids using two thousand banned ingredients that have been banned outside of the US in their products and are fully sustainable. They didn't just want to sell their products, they wanted to educate people to make more informed choices in their day-to-day decisions about what they put on their bodies. We launched a "clean beauty bus" campaign, where people could walk through a Biossance experience and learn about the toxic ingredients found in many common beauty products. We educated their audience about what makes Biossance different and inspired visitors to change the way they think about their own product decisions.[13]

Critical engagement consists of a desire to change. At Level Six, you feel motivated, inspired, and empowered; you are in a position where you are willing to set goals to change for the better.

Critical engagement requires that you consistently ensure that all the lower levels of engagement are being met. If you have reached a point where you inspired someone to change and they are now willing to transform their life, but then you stop acknowledging or responding to them, or you completely change your identity, the whole process fails. I've seen instances where businesses completely change their marketing to connect with a different generation only to have their existing customer base wonder

---

13   "Biossance," CatalystCreativ, https://www.catalystcreativ.com/biossance-clean-beauty-bus.

what's going on. They've been loyal all this time, and they're now being ignored. That's something to avoid!

Level Six is also a time to publicly share your core values that set your culture and distinguish you from competitors.[14] It's about doubling down and ensuring you are living by the values you communicate. Make sure you are authentically aligned with your Seventh Level Statement when identifying your core values and communicate those core values so they are easily understood. Share your story to inspire others to think differently. Ask yourself how your core values not only express what you stand for but also can change the way others think about themselves. Create a campaign around those core values to change the way people think about their own lives.

For example, someone who doesn't wear Patagonia clothes but is environmentally aware might have come across a campaign that Patagonia ran to promote a petition to save a national park from an oil pipeline. They are then inspired to increase their level of activism and political participation and decided to get involved. After that experience, they then become a brand advocate for Patagonia because the brand inspired them to do more about something they cared about.

---

14   "A Guide to Defining Your Company Values," Culture IQ, https://cultureiq.com/blog/defining-company-values/.

Think about how you're communicating the goals you set to get where you are and then come up with a strategy that ensures you're covering Levels One through Five when determining those values. This is so important when it comes to marketing and advertising, but even more important is that you believe it and are doing it internally to transform your own organization—this is not a marketing stunt. Today is the age of transparency. If you're going to market something at this level, make sure you're walking the walk internally. Companies can no longer hide behind products and marketing. Whatever you're selling, your internal goals must match your marketing message.

For example, Zappos's core values center around delighting customers and celebrating entrepreneurship. Customer service and business innovation are baked into everything Zappos does—from how it presents itself publicly, to how it structures itself internally. Zappos's core values are even used in determining individual employee success. Are employees actively seeking to grow the company? Are they customer-focused in their attempts to grow the company?

Your cultural code or internal core values inform how you communicate with your internal and external customers and showcase what is important to you, what you stand for, what you believe in, and what drives you. Imagine being able to share what inspired you (or your company) to change and how you're growing—knowing that it will inspire others to do the same and connect with you in a meaningful way.

This level of engagement requires us to shift away from a corporate infrastructure that has limited us from growth, inspiration, intention, and community building. We need to create a place for feedback—whether from our partners, customers, or employees—and be in a position where we inspire change and growth, or at least a shift in perspective. Not all companies will inspire someone to become an activist, but they can inspire someone to live differently, change their routine, or feel a little bit more strongly about a topic.

IN EXTERNAL CUSTOMERS

How can we inspire others to change? This is where marketing can really come into play.

REI states on their website:

> We believe a life outdoors is better, and we're serious about sharing our passion.

> We're building a thriving community of people who love the outdoors and are giving back to our members, employees and communities.

Their "OptOutside" campaign aligned with their statement. A few years ago, REI decided to close their stores for Black Friday. The purpose behind this move was twofold. They wanted to distance themselves from the consumerism of the day and also give their employees the chance to be outdoors and spend time with their families. They made the decision and shared it with their audience as an #optoutside initiative. It expanded and inspired customers to do the same. REI's following got outdoors and shared the campaign and their stories. The idea started a movement! The company built a website to share stories, they now offer incentive programs, and it was hailed as a massive success. The campaign worked because REI started with their own internal goals. They began with their company's inspiration, and it expanded to inspire others to do the same.

Satya Nadella reevaluated (what I would call) Microsoft's Seventh Level Statement when he became CEO. He didn't change the personal values and beliefs, but he evolved how to communicate those personal values and beliefs with a new Seventh Level Statement that totally transformed the organization from the inside out. The result is a company focused on learning, even if that means making mistakes which permeate throughout the entire organization. He changed the direction Microsoft was headed in and transformed the culture and how to measure the goals set forth by Microsoft—all because of a new "North Star." Microsoft's old Seventh Level Statement just didn't resonate anymore: "A computer on every desk." Using a new Seventh Level Statement—"To empower every person and every organization on the planet to achieve more"—as the lens in which they then determined their internal code of conduct,[15] Microsoft was able to steer its course in a more relevant direction for the modern tech space and the world. While this was meant for his internal customers, it ended up directly impacting the relationship with their external customers, tripling Microsoft's stock price within four years. Microsoft's revamped Seventh Level Statement attracted new attention—and customers—to the established, respected, but perhaps stale brand, and inspired a new generation of people to align with its mission.

By the time you hit the delight phase, you're in a great place. Level Six and the Seventh Level are similar in a lot of ways. At Level Six, you're still asking people to take an action that helps them set goals; Seventh Level customers do it themselves.

Consider Weight Watchers (now called WW) and how it has lasted over the past fifty-plus years. They have always used powerful stories to show how their brand has

---

15   Simone Stolzoff, "How Do You Turn Around the Culture of a 130,000-Person Company? Ask Satya Nadella," *Quartz at Work*, February 1, 2019, https://qz.com/work/1539071/how-microsoft-ceo-satya-nadella-rebuilt-the-company-culture/amp/.

changed people's lives and allowed them to do what they love through losing weight. But now, WW is no longer just about weight loss, it's about holistic health and feeling your best so you can do whatever you love while loving yourself. WW inspires people to set goals to transform their lives. They've partnered with Oprah because their values and beliefs are aligned. Oprah is an actual customer who has seen real results from WW and has been critically engaged at Level Six. The Oprah partnership is authentic for customers, and she was celebrated as a member of the community. This inspired her to become one of WW's largest stakeholders: because of her belief in what WW has done for her and can do for others. Her brand has never been more aligned with WW's. Through aligning with Oprah's story, WW inspires others to set goals and transform as Oprah used WW to set goals and transform themselves. As WW's narrative has evolved, so has how it talks about itself, but at its core, the same values WW was founded on remain just as integral to the organization today.

Your Seventh Level Statement may iterate and evolve a bit over time too. Checking in with yourself is crucial to remaining connected to an ever-evolving world. While your identity does not change, the way you express it very well may need to.

Testimonials are a huge part of Level Six: How did someone's life change by using your product? You don't have to be a philanthropic, sustainable brand to inspire others. Maybe you sell mayo—like Hellman's—and you are thinking, "How am I going to inspire someone to set goals in their life and why does that matter?" These stories are an amazing and authentic way for a company to engage with their customers. Take real people interacting with the product and show how it changed them.

ACTIONS, QUESTIONS, GOALS: EXTERNAL CUSTOMERS

ACTION
The Online Mattress Company releases a sleep training program to teach customers about the benefits of sleep. An individual watches a video on Facebook of a customer of the Online Mattress Company who transformed their sleep habits thanks to this program. The individual is inspired by the customer's story and signs up for the program on the company's website.

QUESTIONS
- How is the Online Mattress Company showcasing the real-life stories of people using their products and resources?
- How is the Online Mattress Company inspiring people to use sleep to improve their lives (outside of pushing the use of their product)?

- Have they seen an increase in sales or site traffic after individuals share their stories on social media?
- Does their audience understand that they don't have to purchase from them to have access to these inspiring resources and stories of how to get better sleep?

GOALS
- Create and share a series of free videos on how to transform your sleep habits.
- Highlight and share stories of transformation across all brand channels.

At this level, the Online Mattress Company's goal is to authentically inspire their audience to transform their own lives based on that company's Seventh Level Statement. By developing free content that speaks to the value of better sleep, audiences can engage with the brand at a deeper level. When customers begin to associate the idea that "improved sleep leads to improved health, which means more energy to do the things you love" with this brand, they are in turn inspired by the company to prioritize sleep in their own lives. The company's presence in their lives goes beyond the products that help them achieve that goal.

INTERNAL CUSTOMERS: IN THE WORKPLACE

As mentioned earlier, workplaces are changing and have been changing since something called "the internet" came about. Individual employee expectations shift more rapidly than most institutions can reasonably accommodate, and companies that are structured as a bureaucracy are not set up to engage with employees at Level Six and the Seventh Level.

As I mentioned earlier, modern workplaces should strive for higher levels than the status quo of Level Four because modern employees are looking for more from their workplaces.[16] Sure, they still want fair compensation and comprehensive benefits packages, but they also want a sense of purpose and connection.

It is harder and harder for workplaces to create spaces where workers can simultaneously actually get stuff done (Level Four) and draw inspiration from the goals of the company. I have learned a lot from my business partner, Tony Hsieh, who I would consider a futurist and a pioneer in customer service and corporate culture. Through Tony, I have seen many new ways of thinking about the workplace arise in response to changes in employment dynamics and the expectations from employees. Older methods of employee engagement might not be as effective in today's post-internet world, where employees want higher engagement from their workplaces. So how do

---

16 Sarita Harbour, "Boosting Employee Happiness: 5 Things Employees Value above Salary," *Zenefits*, May 3, 2018, https://www.zenefits.com/blog/5-things-employees-value-more-than-salary/.

we learn from other workplace infrastructures—not just traditional hierarchical ones—and infuse lessons from different successful cultures in our own companies?

We have organizations and an education system that nod back to the Industrial Revolution and somehow expect people to be creative thinkers and entrepreneurial! We have Gen Zers, millennials, and millennial-minded (Baby Boomers/Gen Xers with millennial psychographics) employees all looking for more from work.

Our phones get an update sometimes more than twice a year, but how often are our work structures modified to reflect new needs? Remote workplaces are on the rise, and flexible workplaces have become increasingly common. People don't just want performatively modern workspaces (with Ping-Pong tables and snacks); they want companies with a sense of values and culture and connection. They want to learn and grow as a part of the company. Employers have more of a responsibility to help employees learn than ever before.

A lot of companies, however, don't know how to engage those employees, and they see high turnover, low productivity, low sales, and low recruitment.

As a leader, it's important to be vulnerable and open with your employees. At Level Six, you are inspiring someone to grow and change. At CatalystCreativ, we have created a culture of support and collective aspiration; one example of this is that I once had an employee who said "um" all the time. I told her my own journey and how difficult it was to communicate clearly and slowly, especially in my first job when I was the only woman leading team meetings my first week, and I had to learn quickly.

As a young woman in the workplace, I found that learning and growing was crucial to my success. For me to feel my best and my most confident, I wanted to be able to clearly communicate my words so people could understand and be moved and inspired. When I was a teacher, the first lesson I taught was filmed. When I watched the tape, I was mortified. I was speaking so fast that the kids couldn't keep up and were completely lost—even *I* could barely keep up! I have had to work my whole life to speak more slowly. (I even took speech lessons when I was in first grade because I spoke so fast that it impacted my breathing.)

I explained to her that I wanted her to feel good in her career, wherever she went, even after CatalystCreativ. I wanted her to be heard, listened to, and respected because her words were valued and smart but were being interrupted all of the time because of "um."

I told her she should want to better these skills for her

own future growth. She understood. She responded and said that my conversation helped her because I showed her my own growth and reasons for wanting her to grow in a professional capacity. I was open and honest with my experiences and why I wanted her to change, and she grew as a result. She saw the long-term opportunity.

This is how we lead from a Level Six engagement.

ACTION, QUESTIONS, GOALS: INTERNAL CUSTOMERS

ACTION
Employees feel a connection to the company's core values and start to adapt them to their personal lives.

QUESTIONS
- What are the company's core values?
- How are they sharing their values? Internally and externally?
- Are their values relatable?
- Are they showing pride in their values (i.e., posting about them online, painting on the wall, printing cards for employees)?
- Do they "live" their own values in everything they do?

GOALS

- Establish a list of core values that align with your company's Seventh Level Statement.
- Provide an opportunity for employees to participate in the development of those values.
- Share those core values with all employees.
- Plan exercises to explain each core value and provide examples of how each value relates to the work the company does.
- Build a platform for employees to share examples and stories of how they and their team embody the core values.

At this level, the leadership team's goal is to inspire their workforce to feel connected to and live by the core values espoused by the organization. (It goes without saying, but this will only happen if your company's values are worth embodying—and gets back to your Seventh Level Statement being of the utmost importance!) Once employees feel deeply aligned with your company, it is important to regularly nurture that inspiration and foster even deeper engagement by continuing to "live" and strive for those core values in the actions the company takes. Then take opportunities to commend exemplary employees who live those values, to continue to inspire others to do the same.

THE CONCEPT OF SELF-ORGANIZATION AND LEVEL SIX ENGAGEMENT

The workplace is being asked to evolve. Conventional bureaucracies are not the end-all, be-all solution to governing a company. Level Six is all about inspiring growth and change, and stale, traditional workplaces are inherently rigid and uncompromising. People are looking for new and nontraditional approaches to creating businesses with a sense of purpose that inspires employees. Moving toward a more self-organized workplace structure is a great way to strive for this Sixth Level of engagement in the workplace. As you work to move beyond Levels Four and Five with your employees, evolving your organization's structure from a traditional, rigid hierarchy to one that encourages employees to take ownership over their careers is crucial.

My own company has been self-organized for six years. We've found that self-organization allows for employees to be more active participants in helping to move the company forward.

That said, self-organization isn't the exact answer for everyone. It does not have to replace the structures you have in place if they are working for you, but lessons from self-organization can still be used to enhance your current workplace environment. (For instance, the sort of self-organization that we employ is based on a concept called "holacracy," but we've modified it to make it our own. You can read more about holacracy and self-organization in books like *Reinventing Organizations*, *The Origin of Wealth*, *Holacracy*, and *Super Cooperators*.)

Self-organization at its core connotes a nonvertical power hierarchy. Employees don't always answer to a supervisor or manager, and work in small circles rather than massive departments. For example, at CatalystCreativ, we have a marketing circle, an event circle, a design circle, and so on. Each act as an almost distinct business, and each uses the Seventh Level Engagement Framework to inform their "business." Within those circles, there is a lead link—essentially the department head but with more freedom and flexibility—and several other roles. The key is that these roles are not necessarily based on who is in the company but rather what the company needs. This means that people perform the roles most essential to the success of the company instead of the ones arbitrarily designated by their title.

We keep track of the roles and accountabilities in our organization. For instance, a company may have a hundred roles but only eight people. Once you identify the roles, you can fill them and then identify gaps. I often see companies hire someone to do one job only to demand they do nine other jobs that weren't specifically outlined in their job description or that they don't get credit for, which is detrimental to engagement—who wants to feel overworked and underappreciated? Clearly defining roles and accountabilities provides accountability, gives people more credit for the work they do, and helps them set goals for themselves as well as the company—all of which are boons to engagement.

To further enhance employee engagement, meetings are based around addressing individual and circle-wide needs, and all employees are equally encouraged to speak up. The ultimate goal of these sessions is to give workers a voice as they strive to push the company forward and to ensure their needs are met so they can do just that. When given the room to perform their jobs in the way they feel most in control and empowered, they feel engaged and ready to transform the organization for the better.

MOVING PAST LEVEL SIX

These higher levels involve different cognitive abilities, and we want engagement that reflects that. We want workplaces that are empathetic, compassionate, and nurturing. We want employees to be the same, but they can't get there if we don't create the infrastructure first.

At this point, you've inspired someone to change, to grow, and to establish goals. Moving them to the Seventh Level is the last piece. It's getting them to think about their existence, their values, and their purpose on the planet. You want someone thinking about whether or not they are making a significant change in others' lives. You want to move them from passivity to activity. You want to catalyze them to be their best self.

You know what makes people tick and what inspires them, but you also really want to personally connect with them so their engagement moves to the next level—they want to identify with your brand, create meaning from your brand, and organically want to share with others—both from a customer and employee level.

By the time you reach Level Six, you should be figuring out ways to maintain this engagement. You have inspired someone, and they are passionate about your brand and want to be a brand advocate. You need to bring them to the next level and keep them there.

The final, Seventh Level takes many of the concepts pertinent to Level Six but makes them more reciprocal. Create opportunities to share your love for these highly engaged customers, and also make it easy for these customers to share their love for you as a proud brand advocate. Doing so can help you elevate them to the Seventh Level and keep them there.

Chapter Eight

THE SEVENTH LEVEL: LITERATE THINKING

I'M IN LOVE

At the film's conclusion, after both Harry and Sally begin their New Year's Eve dateless, a distraught Harry barges into the party Sally is sadly attending.

"I love you," Harry tells Sally.

She initially demurs, suggesting he's just making this gesture now because he's lonely on a day that's hard on lonely people. In response, he begins citing all the idiosyncrasies he loves about her.

"I love that you get cold when it's 71 degrees out. I love that it takes you an hour and a half to order a sandwich. I love that you get a little crinkle above your nose when you're looking at me like I'm nuts. I love that after I spend the day with you, I can still smell your perfume on my clothes. And I love that you are the last person I want to talk to before I go to sleep at night. And it's not because I'm lonely, and it's not because it's New Year's Eve. I came here tonight because when you realize you want to spend the rest of your life with somebody, you want the rest of your life to start as soon as possible."

"You see?" Sally replies, stunned. "That is just like you, Harry. You say things like that, and you make it impossible for me to hate you."

At this point Harry and Sally inspire each other to be their best selves, and there's a deep, mutual understanding between them. It took the journey to the Seventh Level for them both to be in this relationship. It took understanding their own personal beliefs and narratives. It required having an identity and standing up for love.

And that's the Seventh Level: a direct alignment of personal beliefs that leads to loyalty and action without incentive. Of course, the film concludes with Harry asking Sally to marry him. If that's not emblematic of loyalty stemming from direct alignment of personal beliefs, then what is?

What was the last rom-com that showed you the work it took to maintain that love after the happy ending? That is also the value of the Seventh Level Engagement Framework—doing the work to maintain the loyalty and advocacy and not taking your audience for granted.

Of course, for this example to truly work as emblematic of the Seventh Level, we have to assume that this delightful, yet unlikely rom-com couple continues to put in the work necessary to keep their love from growing stale and their ability to inspire one another from wilting.

THE HOLY GRAIL OF ENGAGEMENT

Everything from the workplace to marketing to the way we connect has changed because of the internet. We can share about our lives all the time, and we can know small details about the brands we support. Brands can share about their leaders and values as much as they can about their products and services. Loyalty doesn't stop at a purchase. People now more than ever think of their personal brand, and part of their identity comes from the brands they use. It becomes a part of you. Customers deriving meaning from the experience, as we have discussed, a simple purchase from REI can become part of your identity. At this level, a customer moves from Level Six to the Seventh Level.

Literate thinking is when your audience's values and beliefs line up with your message. When I was a child, it was hard for me to sit still and read. I always preferred to socialize over sitting down to read a book, but then I was introduced to *Matilda*. I was so inspired by her tenacity and her ability to overcome anything that was thrown at her that I identified with her and became an avid reader like her. I became the top reader in second grade because her character spoke to me viscerally and woke something up in me.

The world of storytelling and content is far different than it was during my childhood. We are bombarded by content, writing, words, images, and videos all the time. How can brands that strive for Seventh Level engagement connect meaningfully, deeply, and emotionally with their customers? At this level, stories are crucial. And what's a stronger storytelling medium than something that is near and dear to my own—and my childhood bestie Matilda's— heart than books?

Books are a significant part of the Seventh Level. I recently spoke to Gabriela Periera who runs a program called DIY MFA.[17] She said that research into neural brain

17   DIY MFA, www.diymfa.com.

activity shows that when you are reading a book, you have higher brain functions than while participating in other activities. You envision the character and put yourself in the character's shoes, imagining the scene using different parts of your brain than if you watch a television show or a movie. Having your mind in a book is a Seventh Level of engagement in terms of engaging yourself. Have you ever felt so sad after a book was over because you feel like you just lost your best friend? You feel deeply connected to the characters as if they are a part of you.

Tony Hsieh is a fairly shy person who does not open up to just anyone, but he comes to life in his book, sharing his Seventh Level Statement of delivering happiness by inspiring, connecting, educating, and entertaining throughout his whole story. The books he's authored have helped build brand loyalty for the multiple projects he believes in because people know what he stands for. Brené Brown, noted for what I could consider her Seventh Level Statement about the power of vulnerability in leadership, has created a cultlike following, one of the most watched TED Talks of all time, and even a Netflix special. Her success at connecting with people is not only because she is a great researcher but because of how she has built a business around what she stands for, believes in, and communicates to the world.

Learning from longer format storytelling mediums—like

books—is crucial for highly engaged customers. Thought leaders know that sharing in long-form on LinkedIn and in books leads to higher-level engagement. For example, one of our clients, Speakfully, offers a platform to manage, measure, and support people who have experienced workplace mistreatment. I reshared a post on LinkedIn about the founder's personal story and her inspiration for founding the platform. People saw themselves in her story, and because of that, this post became a top trending workplace post.

At this level, it is about including your customers in your story and making them the hero. Amplify their narratives and highlight how they reflect your own. Make them feel special, seen, and heard, and they'll carry what you're doing forward. Companies announce exclusive offers, launch experiences, and new products to Seventh Level customers the day before the general public as a "thank you" for being loyal. This also activates Seventh Level customers to bring other customers up from lower levels.

When speaking to the journalist—and my dear friend—Cal Fussman on his podcast, we discussed a new company that has Seventh Level fans in New Zealand and Australia, and plans to launch in America. I told Cal that this company should work with their already existing brand advocates to connect with a new market rather than doing all the work themselves. This brand's

Kiwi and Australian audiences can demonstrate to newer American audiences that this is a brand worth not only paying attention to but becoming passionate about. That endorsement can do more for this expanding company's short-term success in a new market than almost any more conventional campaign ever could.

Engagement influences attention, sentiment, and time—our greatest resource that we routinely give away freely.

We started the book with defining your Seventh Level Statement, which is your natural guide for this whole process and a lens through which you connect with others. Your Seventh Level is your North Star. Your guiding force. You identified yourself, you worked through the levels, and now you're ready for a commitment—whether it's from a partner, a customer, or an employee. These are your most loyal engagements. It's time to thank them for being a part of your story. People who connect with you at this level are true, steadfast, deep, and connect with who you really are, not who you pretend to be.

This is what you are, and you've connected with someone from that place, someone gets you, you're aligned, and you can help each other.

Literate thinking combines trust, effort, affirmation,

inspiration, pride, loyalty, and should evoke a feeling of *we did this together!*

IN EXTERNAL CUSTOMERS

When I first started in events and marketing, the first event I ever produced was for Harley-Davidson. They wanted to do something to include the media in the journey, not just a traditional event with passive consumers gawking at the bikes. They wanted to communicate their Seventh Level Statement of freedom for all. We created an experience with Harley-Davidson motorcycles in the venue but also had Harley-Davidson motorcycles you could actually ride around the city (with a license of course). We had a temporary tattoo artist on one side for those who are a bit less brave and a permanent tattoo artist on the other (with a ton of waivers). Harley-Davidson goes the extra mile in the way they show up for their fans. They create experiences that don't just passively entertain but actively engage and delight, and this event was no exception.

You can find literally millions of search results on Google for Harley-Davidson tattoos. People aren't tattooing a logo: they are tattooing something they stand for and believe in. It's an expression of freedom and an obsession for many.

Even if you have a customer at the Seventh Level, there

are still a million distractions (opportunities for frustrated engagement, if you will) in the world. It's important that you create a pathway for people to stay committed, which means that you have to also be committed to them. One idea toward maintaining your customer base is to build a loyalty or retention program. Talk to them differently. Consider building a sales and outreach team that works on a personalized marketing approach.

At this level, it is not about referral codes or financial incentives. (Remember, that is Level Five). It is about emotionally incentivizing your customers by making them feel special. It could be giving them access to behind-the-scenes photos from a photoshoot or telling them about a launch before the public knows. Maybe it's featuring them in a campaign or their personal narratives on your website. Maybe it's sending them something that is personal to them or taking your most loyal customers on a trip. It is not "Do this, and get this," it is "You have done this without us asking, and we notice you. You are seen, you are heard, and we are grateful." If you aren't careful to maintain this loyalty, frustrated engagement can happen quickly.

When we were doing Catalyst Weeks, we would partner with brands that would use the experience as an incentive for their most loyal employees and followers. They would "co-curate the week" by sponsoring the experience and inviting their fifteen most loyal Seventh Level customers to attend the three-day experience to show them their gratitude.

If you've had someone as a customer for ten years, don't send them the same email as if they've been with you for one year. Ever buy a ticket to your favorite music festival four years in a row only to get an email that says "Purchase a ticket" after you already purchased one? What! Do they even know you at all!? You feel slighted and certainly not valued. This is because you don't feel seen, you feel taken for granted, and lumped in with any other person just passively considering attending the festival. This is about not just saying, "I love you," but listing all the ways you love someone, just like Harry to Sally. Segment out your audience and personalize the messages. Show your gratitude. Make the customer the hero in your narrative by shining a light on them and letting them take center stage in your stories and communications. Make them feel special!

This may seem like a lot of work, but it's less work than the alternative! If you are already doing all of this in a disjointed way, seeing what sticks but without a plan, then every time you lose the attention of your customers or connect with them briefly only to disconnect them, you are making it harder for yourself the next time.

To reach the Seventh Level, and keep your audience there,

it *is* a lot of work. But this relationship—and your job—will get easier, not harder, over time, the more energy and effort you put into it. That's because at Level Seven, you are cultivating brand advocates who can spread your message just as effectively as you can! So keep them engaged. Make sure they feel appreciated for caring about you. Make sure they know you care about them. Don't ask them to buy a ticket to your event when they have your logo tattooed on their arm. Don't ask for that first date if they are already married to you!

ACTION, QUESTIONS, GOALS:
EXTERNAL CUSTOMERS

ACTION

A customer of the Online Mattress Company voluntarily and consistently shares on their personal channels how their mattress purchase has transformed their life and becomes an advocate for the brand. They tag friends and tell everyone they know to buy a mattress because they are so in love with the brand.

QUESTIONS

- How is the company providing value for the people that are telling their story?
- What special recognition would individuals get by associating with the Online Mattress Company?

- What are they offering these customers as long-term benefits so they never buy from another company again?
- How are they making it easy for customers to refer friends?
- How is the Online Mattress Company making it easy for customers to share their stories with them?
- How is the Online Mattress Company engaging with the people that are sharing their stories about their product across public channels?
- Is there a hashtag that the company uses so that people can follow along with the inspiring customer stories being shared and foster a greater sense of belonging?

GOALS

- Connect directly and interact with every individual who shares their own stories publicly and privately.
- Develop a social media engagement strategy and position staff to be ready to respond to individuals personally.
- Highlight the stories digitally, making the Seventh Level customer the "hero" on the company blog and/or social channels.
- Develop a top-tier "sleep anniversary" loyalty program to make these customers feel special for life.
- Launch a referral program.

At this level, the Online Mattress Company should prioritize attending to those customers who have reached the highest level of engagement. Developing programs to acknowledge, nurture, and maintain relationships with these customers is key, as they will continue to advocate for the brand as long as they are at this level. It might require some extra effort to launch a referral program or send handwritten thank-you notes to top customers, but maintaining Level Seven relationships is what separates the world's most beloved brands from those people forget about.

INTERNAL CUSTOMERS: IN THE WORKPLACE

A Seventh Level company is one that fully embodies the beliefs and purpose they've established—both internally and externally. At the Seventh Level, employees are personally connected to the purpose—not only to the benefits or how much they're getting paid. Employees don't work at the "top places to work" companies because they have good health insurance. They work there because they are personally connected to the identity of the organization because of what the company stands for and does on a daily basis.

Consider the following quotes about companies that operate from their Seventh Level Statements. You'll notice the employees are not describing their health benefits or how great their bonus structure is. They are talking about what it means to work at these companies, how their Seventh Level Statements collide:

"The company is committed to learning and innovating—keen to try new things, and always ready to support new ideas."

SALESFORCE QUOTE FROM FORTUNE 100[18]

"Working for this company instills a sense of purpose. The Wegman family and all executives and leaders are engaged, invested, and committed to our mission of helping people live healthier, better lives through food, and in doing the right thing."

WEGMAN'S QUOTE FROM FORTUNE 100[19]

"Besides the amazing benefits we receive here every day, any time an Ultipeep or their family member is in need or passes away, the company pulls together to show an outpouring of love and support like I have never seen elsewhere."

ULTIMATE SOFTWARE QUOTE FROM FORTUNE 100[20]

As a leader, use the Seventh Level by making your employees the hero. Promote them to the world; show them you appreciate them! They are the bedrock of your organization.

---

18 "Fortune 100 Best Companies to Work for 2018," Great Place to Work Institute, 2018, https://www.greatplacetowork.com/best-workplaces/100-best/2018.

19 "Fortune 100 Best Companies."

20 "Fortune 100 Best Companies."

You know you've reached the Seventh Level when you have people who identify with your company and make it their own "personal brand." They want to share on your behalf, without you asking, because it also defines their own sense of self.

ACTION, QUESTIONS, GOALS: INTERNAL CUSTOMERS

ACTION

An employee becomes a brand ambassador, not only telling others about the amazing products/services they offer but going as far as to refer the company to their friends seeking employment or the services the company provides.

QUESTIONS

- How is the company aligning their employee's Seventh Level Statements with their own to build the company culture collaboratively?
- What are they offering these employees beyond financial incentives, in long-term emotional benefits, so they remain loyal to the company?
- How are they making it easy for these employees to share about the company and what it stands for?

GOALS

- Launch an employee appreciation program in which the company highlights employees who are brand ambassadors.
- Provide employee brand ambassadors a platform on which to share their passion and ideas.
- Increase employee goal-setting and company follow-through—build pride in achieving goals and company growth.
- Identify a way to guide potential employees in finding their own Seventh Level Statements during the interview process.
- Only sign contracts with people/companies that align with the company's Seventh Level Statement.

At the Seventh Level, a company should be prioritizing making its top-performing and most bought-in employees feel appreciated for their hard work and dedication to the organization's goals and values. In doing so, the company continues to prove itself to be a great place to work and also maintains a top-notch relationship with its employees most likely to go above and beyond—and recruit more Seventh Level talent via referrals. One way to accomplish this is to create an ambassador program that enables Seventh Level employees to travel to events or recruiting sessions on behalf of the company, which provides them with a platform to speak to their experiences, shows they're appreciated and respected, and gives them a fun opportunity to represent and engage with the company in new ways.

WORKING TO STAY AT THE SEVENTH LEVEL

When Harry Met Sally... remains a classic to this day because it's well written, funny, and believable. Accordingly, Harry and Sally don't continually "level up" their relationship. There are hills and valleys along the way—and that's how engagement works too. It takes a lot of work to cultivate engagement all the way to the Seventh Level, and just as much to keep people up there—the journey isn't always smooth, but since Seventh Level engagers are truly the driving force behind your brand, it's always worth it.

Once you get to the Seventh Level, the challenge is keeping your audience there. The worst thing you could do is let them loose, go dark, or fail to give them support. It's okay for them to slide down a level or two; that's fixable. It's going to happen. But if you make sure your audience continues to feel seen and heard, you'll create those deep connections that we all want.

STAND BEHIND YOUR MESSAGE

Once you have your message, you can change the way you frame something, but you can't change who you are as that will cause you to lose your Seventh Level customers. How do you use branding as a mechanism to show people you are passionate about them? At CatalystCreativ, we created a campaign asking people for Seventh Level

Statements with #myseventhlevel, and we are creating beautiful visuals/quotes that we send to those people and share from our own social to show that they matter to us.[21]

Going the extra step and developing custom graphics and branding make people feel seen, especially when you share it on your own social. It also makes them want to share it as well. After we posted one woman's Seventh Level Statement, she responded by saying:

> Omg! You made my day and completely shook up my professional self! 🙌 Everything I do is now with the Seven Levels in mind. 🙃 Thank You!

We do the same thing with beautiful case studies on our website and wrap up reports for our clients, showing them the work that was completed with a beautiful time-intensive presentation that we put together to celebrate the work we have done with them.

Writing this book dovetails with my Seventh Level—I want to educate and inspire people and hope I've done that for you. I believe in this framework; it's what I stand for and am passionate about. That's why my company, CatalystCreativ, has won business over the past years.

---

21   "What Is a Seventh Level Statement," *The Seventh Level*, May 13, 2019, https://blog. catalystcreativ.com/what-is-a-seventh-level-statement.

I don't want to tell you about our services; you can see that on the website. I do want you to know that we started in 2012, but we're still growing and figuring out how to communicate our identity to the world. We are not a traditional brand/marketing consultancy; we need to continue to stand for something, as we are competing for business with thousands of other companies. We won't get clients or talent if we don't stand for something—so similar to my personal Seventh Level Statement, we as a company have a goal of turning passive consumers into active participants by inspiring and educating them. We use the Seventh Level Engagement Framework to change the way that people look at themselves and the world. That's the message we stand behind.

A CAMPAIGN FROM LEVEL ONE
TO THE SEVENTH LEVEL

You might be wondering what each level of the Seventh Level Engagement Framework looks like as applied to a specific campaign. The 2018 Nike Kaepernick campaign is a great example of a company that applied the Seventh Level Engagement Framework. Whether you loved or hated it, it caused a visceral reaction. The issues were not a mistake or an experiment. It was strategic because Nike was losing customers and athletes to brands like Adidas and Under Armour. They had to put their stake in the ground and stand up for something. They decided to give up a ton of mediocre customers that were at Level Four or Five in order to keep their Seventh Level customers. They didn't care if they lost some customers, who ended up burning their shoes. Some of these lower-level-engaged customers were outraged, they were disgusted, and frustrated engaged; they were distracted, and so they took photos and videos of themselves burning their Nike shoes. But Nike was not after those people's loyalty. They were after maintaining the loyalty from their true customers, for what they really stood for. At the end of the day, regardless if it was bad or good, people talked about it.

Nike created a viral moment. They were okay with losing support because they started with their Seventh Level Statement: "Just do it," which they expanded to "Believe in something, even if it means sacrificing everything." Let's pretend for a moment that we are sitting at the table at Nike during the conception of the campaign to better understand the journey:

- Level One: Who and where are your customers?

Our target audience is the socially conscious sports fan. That sort of person is everywhere, but they are the easiest to identify and target on social media.

- Level Two: What are you saying and how are you saying it?

Directly nodding to Kaepernick's activism might be too polarizing. We need to express that he sacrificed a lot financially and socially by standing up for what he believed in, but in a broad enough way that others can relate, regardless of their perspective on the issue his protests have drawn attention to.

- Level Three: How are we creating the customer journey to move it from frustrated engagement?

We're going to make sure that the campaign is at the Super Bowl, on our social media channels, and that we are controlling the narrative so that it's not distracting. (They identified a proper user journey.)

- Level Four: How do we provide structure-dependent engagement?

We're going to slowly tease it out and ask people to comment. We will respond, retweet their interaction, and have them be a part of it.

- Level Five: How do we build self-regulated interest?

We identify the athletes that will stand for this message and leverage them in a meaningful, powerful way.

- Level Six: How do we inspire?

We want them to think about something differently, to transform their lives, to stand for something.

- It all resulted in Level Seven—a personal narrative and identity that allowed fans to personally connect with Nike again.

AN EVENT FROM LEVEL ONE TO
THE SEVENTH LEVEL

When CatalystCreativ's own event mastermind, Robert, planned his gorgeous wedding outside of Knoxville, Tennessee, to his awesome—now husband!—Anthony, we couldn't help but look at the process through the lens of our Seventh Level Engagement Framework. Everything from the proposal (at least on an *engagement* pun level), to the planning, to the execution of Robert and Anthony's perfect day, can be better understood when analyzed this way.

Orchestrating the perfect wedding is clearly a massive undertaking, but it's an accumulation of tiny details, executed to perfection, that makes the day truly special and memorable for guests and betrothed alike. And by considering possible steps where guests might feel left out, neglected, distracted, or confused, and proactively ensuring those things never happened, Robert and Anthony's wedding day was the perfect celebration—and encapsulation—of their love.

- **Level One: Disengagement**—suppose that after invitations were sent out, someone didn't RSVP to their wedding. They'd be avoiding or idle from the task at hand.

This of course, wasn't an issue for R+A, who took extra precautions to ensure that guests were being informed and nudged at all the right steps of the process. They set up and sent out links to an online portal with an easy-to-navigate digital experience, containing all the necessary information prior to the save-the-dates going out. They next sent a save-the-date far enough out so that guests could keep their calendars clear. Lastly, they made sure guests received their invitations by hand-delivering them locally so they wouldn't get ruined, lost, or delayed in the mailing process.

- **Level Two: Unsystematic Engagement (confusion over messaging)**—If you've ever organized a big event, you know Level Two is a major hurdle to jump over. People ask a million questions when participating in something new or unfamiliar.

Robert and Anthony had a destination wedding, and foresaw unsystematic engagement being a potential issue. They knew that laying out a clear, detailed plan was crucial. So—with the help of Mike Mason, CatalystCreativ's creative director—they created a series of attractive, printed assets, giving guests the information they'd need around their arrival. These were included in welcome bags for all guests, and daily printed schedules were handed out each morning at breakfast.

- **Level Three: Frustrated Engagement**—People tend to be distracted at this level. They have a ton going on besides attending a wedding.

Robert and Anthony clearly laid out not only the logistics for the weekend, but their expectations as well (no sense having a guest worry about whether their outfit is sufficiently formal). Driving directions, expected weather, and a list of phone numbers to call with any questions were provided. They made it as simple as possible to be present by ensuring the logistics of the wedding were not an additional distraction.

- **Level Four: Structure-dependent Engagement**—At this level, people are likely to engage with an event, as long as the barrier to entry is low.

Robert does events for a living. He knows that when groups of four or more gather, they want to be told what to do. Guests arriving early were invited to an informal but still structured dinner their first night. Robert spoke to everyone who would be in town for the dinner and had them all make reservations within the same time frame to allow for some flexibility but also to make sure they'd be in the same place at the same time. Guests felt tended to, appreciated, and ready to enjoy the rest of the weekend.

- **Level Five: Self-regulated Interest**—This example is less applicable for a wedding, as guests come out of love, but R+A didn't want to take advantage of that fact too much.

They knew a lot of guests were coming from out of town and that finding a hair or makeup person far from home can be tough. To make sure distant travelers felt appreciated and excited about looking good for the big day, Robert and Anthony arranged for anyone who wanted to have their hair and makeup done.

- **Level Six: Critical Engagement**—Here people are inspired to make a change in their own lives.

For the ceremony itself, Robert and Anthony included passages that were meaningful to them, like an excerpt from Justice Anthony Kennedy's majority opinion that legalized gay marriage in the United States. They also incorporated Jewish traditions like stomping the glass for Anthony, and Christian traditions like Bible verses, read by Robert's brother.

- **Seventh Level**, direct alignment of personal beliefs: Lastly, Robert and Anthony wanted guests—even those not related to them—to leave feeling like family: connected, loved, and part of a beautiful experience. Robert and Anthony wrote personalized cards to everyone in attendance, expressing the importance of each person to them. Additionally, Robert's grandfather had recently passed, so handkerchiefs monogrammed with his initials and sewn with a small piece of his favorite tie were given out to family at the rehearsal dinner.

CONCLUSION

SEVENTH LEVEL RETURNS

This is the age of attention. Advertising is at an all-time saturation point. We need loyal fan bases to cut through the clutter of what is currently a mess of messaging. Keeping people loyal is so much harder today, given the unprecedented number of options people are presented daily. When you reach Seventh Level with a subset of your customers, keep them there and help them help you.

When you reach the Seventh Level, you'll see massive returns. Think of Salesforce, a company that went public in 2004 but brought in an estimated $13.3 billion in revenue in 2019. Ninety-seven percent of surveyed Salesforce employees feel good about their company's contributions to the community, 95 percent think company management is honest and ethical, and 95 percent are proud to tell others where they work. From a company perspective, you have long-term sustainability, customer retention, and brand ambassadors. You've moved passive consumers into active participants and have an audience of brand loyalists who are sharing your message. Once you have reached the Seventh Level, there's not as much work because your loyal followers do it for you! They are giving you money for your product, but they are also giving you time and attention—and they need to be rewarded for that.

Bosses and employers see employee retention and increased productivity. Your employees are out cheering you on, and it's that much easier to bring in business. You don't have to ask them to share, they do it on their own. They talk about the company and try to bring in sales even when out of the office. And they recruit for you—top talent attracts top talent. And as you can imagine, a company that hires and keeps the sort of person who makes sales because they believe in what they are doing and whose positive outlook on work basically serves as an extension of your PR team's efforts, is a company that thrives. Simply put, Seventh Level Engagement with your team leads to improved ROI—return on investment *and* ripple of impact.

APPLY IT ACROSS THE BOARD

It's my dream to see the Seventh Level Engagement Framework integrated into all departments across all companies. As you've learned, engagement is so much more than what you thought. Engagement is not just marketing, likes, or employee relations—it's meaningful connections that lead to increased achievement.

It impacts sales, human resources, management, and your bottom line. If you've built connections with your team—use the Seventh Level Engagement Framework across your entire organization. If you used it and tested it on your marketing, now apply it to your employee relations and sales team. Look at the way you're onboarding customers, and really leverage this framework as a road map for everything that you're doing.

Use the Framework in your planning. Use it when you introduce a new concept to the organization. Use it when you're trying to market a concept internally to the company. Use it when you're conducting employee reviews. Once you've gone through the process in one aspect of your life, you can easily adapt it to others. The more you use the Framework, the more natural it becomes and the more it influences your natural thought process when confronted with a challenge. You'll find yourself thinking more deeply and deliberately about the nature of your connections to your friends, family, peers, and customers, and approaching these interactions with greater intentions.

We all have different definitions of engagement. Let this be the common denominator in your company so your sales, marketing, design, HR, are using the same wave of success in the company.

You know your Seventh Level Statement at your core, but be sure to frequently revisit those first levels. Make sure you know your audience, how you're talking to them, and when you're talking to them. Your customers and their needs will evolve and change. Recognize what you stand for and communicate that value to them; as their needs may change, your products may be modernized, but you stay true to who you are.

After you've completed this framework, it becomes easy to identify where others are in their relationship with you. You can start to segment people and recognize their current levels. Once you know that, and where you'd like to take them, it's easier to progress through the steps.

So many of us stumble around in the dark. We are in relationships where we bump up against one another with no idea how to further connect. We don't understand the other person's reactions or why we react in turn. The Seventh Level Engagement Framework is a flashlight shining light on how to build connections that can be used in every part of your life.

START WITH YOUR OWN SEVENTH LEVEL STATEMENT

I can't reiterate this enough. To live the life you want, you have to know your Seventh Level before you jump into a relationship, before you jump into a job, before you jump into anything! Know yourself and your goals, and that will determine what a meaningful connection looks like for you.

This North Star becomes your guiding light and allows for relationships that are more meaningful, stronger, and sustainable than you ever thought possible. Imagine a world of engaged citizens, of engaged families, of engaged husbands and wives, of engaged students, of engaged employees, of engaged customers.

We would have a world of inspired, active participants doing their part to make the world better than when they came to it. Let's strive for a more engaged planet, starting with the Seventh Level.

APPENDIX

CASE STUDIES

THE ONLINE MATTRESS COMPANY EXAMPLE

LEVEL ONE: ACTION, QUESTIONS, GOALS: EXTERNAL CUSTOMERS

ACTION

The Online Mattress Company runs a series of Instagram ads to drive traffic to their website. The audience is scrolling past the ads without clicking.

QUESTIONS
- What do their current customers look like?
- Where does their target audience spend time online?
- Are their ads on the right platform?
- Are they targeting the right audience?

GOALS

- Evaluate existing customer base.
- Identify the top two "types" of current customers that most often purchase.
- Identify one to two "types" of aspirational customers that they'd like to target.

The Online Mattress Company's goal is to use existing customer or aspirational target customer data to create personas that guide future ad targeting. The research focuses on demographics and psychographics, including where that "type" of person spends time, what they read, how they consume information, what social channels they use most, etc.

LEVEL TWO: ACTION, QUESTIONS, AND GOALS: EXTERNAL CUSTOMERS

ACTION

A potential customer for the Online Mattress Company visits their website after clicking on an ad, but they are confused by the process of purchasing a mattress online. The customer leaves the company's website without getting past the home page.

QUESTIONS

- Is the company clearly communicating the steps of buying and installing a mattress purchased online?

- How is the Online Mattress Company communicating the benefits of purchasing with them and buying a mattress online versus in-store to their potential customers?
- Has the company tested their messaging about the process of buying a mattress online?

GOALS

- Survey target audiences to understand what their questions and barriers to entry to purchasing a mattress online are.
- Add messaging to the home page that makes it easy to understand the purchase journey for a customer and the value it provides by testing a variety of messaging tools (i.e., visually, video, copy) and see what performs best.
- Review competitor websites and messaging to analyze what they're using to gather insight.

For the Online Mattress Company, trying to attract customers who have never shopped online for a mattress before at this level a goal would be to demystify that experience. One way to do this would be preemptively alleviating any concerns and answering any questions a first-time buyer might have. They should spell out, step by step, what to expect from purchase to setup on their home page as well as incorporate key messaging that highlights the value of choosing this type of direct-to-consumer mattress over a traditional one. These actions are key to helping capture the attention of those who reach their site while at the second level of engagement.

LEVEL THREE: ACTION, QUESTIONS, AND
GOALS: EXTERNAL CUSTOMERS

ACTION

An existing customer of the Online Mattress Company leaves the website without browsing other products after being served with a pop-up offering them a discount for a product they already purchased.

QUESTIONS

- Has the Online Mattress Company mapped out multiple customer journeys for various customer types?
- Do they understand what items people are likely to buy after they buy a mattress?
- Have they set up suitable triggers for various calls to action based on the data they have and/or actions actually taken by customers?

GOALS

- Email purchasers at the established intervals (thirty-, sixty-, ninety-day check-in periods, six to twelve months) and offer ancillary purchase options, such as pillows and sheets.
- Email customers based on purchasing habits (i.e., they have purchased X, so the next email offer is for Y).
- For those site visitors who the Online Mattress Company has previous session/purchase data for, customize the pop-up they are presented when visiting the site. For existing customers, present them with a pop-up discount offer on

ancillary products (i.e., sheets, pillow, etc.). For new visitors, present them with a pop-up discount offer on a new mattress.

- For those site visitors who the Online Mattress Company does not have previous session/purchase data for, offer two pop-up options instead of one specific offer: one for those with a mattress and one for those without. The one the visitor selects will determine which offer they see—a discount to purchase a mattress or a discount to purchase ancillary products.

For Level Three, the Online Mattress Company's goal is to limit distractions when existing or new potential customers visit their website. They can do this by leveraging the technology they have to develop various pop-up user experiences on their website, which all serve to funnel visitors toward a desired outcome. They should ensure a site visitor isn't distracted by a message that is not relevant. Don't bombard people with a variety of requests in a variety of ways. Keep it simple and keep it consistent.

LEVEL FOUR: ACTIONS, QUESTIONS, GOALS: EXTERNAL CUSTOMERS

ACTION
The Online Mattress Company's Instagram followers will comment on the company's posts when they're prompted directly

in the caption.

QUESTIONS

- Is the company using the lens of their Seventh Level Statement to determine what calls to action or social media strategy they are using to elicit comments?
- Are they posting questions with content that is truly of interest to their followers' values and beliefs?
- Has the company looked at competitors and the types of calls to action they are using to engage their followers?
- Has the company analyzed the types of calls to action that have been most successful in eliciting comments in the past?
- Have they been encouraging and responding to the few followers who have shared or commented on their content?

GOALS

- Assign a community manager to monitor and respond to and/or like all post comments.
- Follow up individually with those who share via post as well as direct messages, when appropriate.
- Read comments and show gratitude publicly for followers who have commented in the desired, appropriate way, highlighting conversations aligned with the company's Seventh Level Statement.

At this level, the Online Mattress Company's goal is to engage with its audience by asking they take a small, desired action, then acknowledging that participation in an authentic way. This request should be reasonable and simple for their followers and should contribute to improving the metrics the company is aiming to improve. By the Online Mattress Company showing appreciation for those who comment, they can maintain audience engagement and open the door for future, higher-level engagement as well—this can be something as simple as responding to a comment.

LEVEL FIVE: ACTION, QUESTIONS, GOALS: EXTERNAL CUSTOMERS

ACTION

The Online Mattress Company partners with a celebrity influencer to launch a sweepstakes wherein their audience can enter to win a chance to have that celebrity deliver a new mattress to their house. To enter, the audience must share their personal answer to "what they're driven to do every day—on a good night's sleep" on Instagram.

QUESTIONS

- Have they gathered enough information to confirm that this is an incentive that would be effective with their target audience?
- Is the celebrity influencer promotion connecting with the self-interest of their customers?
- Does this celebrity align with their brand values and beliefs (i.e., their Seventh Level Statement)?

- Are the incentive and incentivized behavior of commiserate value? (i.e., is what's being offered by the company enough for the customer to take action? Is the desired customer action appropriately valuable for the incentive offered?)

GOALS

- Do appropriate research and informal surveying to identify the right celebrity influencer to capture the interest of their target audience.
- Conduct in-depth analysis of what the top five topics this celebrity influencer stands for.
- Analyze the behavior of the celebrity's social media followers, beyond just the size of their audience.
- Ensure that the celebrity influencer is authentically connected to the brand and willing to provide a mutually beneficial messaging and promotional strategy (not just "pay to post").

The Online Mattress Company's goal is to identify what type of incentive this target audience would find most appealing. Level Five is all about "What's in it for me?" and strategically providing an incentive to customers that is authentically aligned with your brand and that of the celebrity/microinfluencer partner.

LEVEL SIX: ACTIONS, QUESTIONS, GOALS: EXTERNAL CUSTOMERS

ACTION

The Online Mattress Company releases a sleep training program to teach customers about the benefits of sleep. An individual watches a video on Facebook of a customer of the Online Mattress Company who transformed their sleep habits thanks to this program. The individual is inspired by the customer's story and signs up for the program on the company's website.

QUESTIONS

- How is the Online Mattress Company showcasing the real-life stories of people using their products and resources?
- How is the Online Mattress Company inspiring people to use sleep to improve their lives (outside of pushing the use of their product)?
- Have they seen an increase in sales or site traffic after individuals share their stories on social media?
- Does their audience understand that they don't have to purchase from them to have access to these inspiring resources and stories of how to get better sleep?

GOALS

- Create and share a series of free videos on how to transform your sleep habits.
- Highlight and share stories of transformation across all brand channels.

At this level, the Online Mattress Company's goal is to authentically inspire their audience to transform their own lives based on that company's Seventh Level Statement. By developing free content that speaks to the value of better sleep, audiences can engage with the brand at a deeper level. When customers begin to associate the idea that "improved sleep leads to improved health, which means more energy to do the things you love" with this brand, they are in turn inspired by the company to prioritize sleep in their own lives. The company's presence in their lives goes beyond the products that help them achieve that goal.

SEVENTH LEVEL: ACTION, QUESTIONS, GOALS: EXTERNAL CUSTOMERS

ACTION

A customer of the Online Mattress Company voluntarily and consistently shares on their personal channels how their mattress purchase has transformed their life and becomes an advocate for the brand. They tag friends and tell everyone they know to buy a mattress because they are so in love with the brand.

QUESTIONS

- How is the company providing value for the people that are telling their story?
- What special recognition would individuals get by associat-

ing with the Online Mattress Company?

- What are they offering these customers as long-term benefits so they never buy from another company again?
- How are they making it easy for customers to refer friends?
- How is the Online Mattress Company making it easy for customers to share their stories with them?
- How is the Online Mattress Company engaging with the people that are sharing their stories about their product across public channels?
- Is there a hashtag that the company uses so that people can follow along with the inspiring customer stories being shared and can foster a greater sense of belonging?

GOALS

- Connect directly and interact with every individual who shares their own stories publicly and privately.
- Develop a social media engagement strategy and position staff to be ready to respond to individuals personally.
- Highlight the stories digitally, making the Seventh Level customer the "hero" on the company blog and/or social channels.
- Develop a top-tier "sleep anniversary" loyalty program to make these customers feel special for life.
- Launch a referral program.

At this level, the Online Mattress Company should prioritize attending to those customers who have reached the highest level of engagement. Developing programs to acknowledge, nurture, and maintain relationships with these customers is key, as they will continue to advocate for the brand as long as they are at this level. It might require some extra effort to launch a referral program or send handwritten thank-you notes to top customers, but maintaining Seventh Level relationships is what separates the world's most beloved brands from those that people forget about.

EMPLOYEE RELATIONS EXAMPLE

LEVEL ONE: ACTION, QUESTIONS, GOALS: INTERNAL CUSTOMERS

ACTION
An HR representative sends out an email to all employees requesting their participation in a new goal-setting program. The employees do not respond to the representative's email.

QUESTIONS
- Have they asked what their employees' preferred method of contact is?
- What time of day did they send the email?
- Did the HR representative send the email to a group or to each individual?
- Was the email successfully delivered to each employee?
- Have they tried reaching out to their employees personally to do an informal survey to ask why they didn't respond?

GOALS

- Establish company-wide communication guidelines and let employees know that they should expect to receive HR requests via email.
- Include links to information and resources related to each request and call them out in the message.
- When an employee is onboarded, ask what their preferred method of communication is.
- Send a follow-up to individual team members via their preferred contact method with a personal message to ensure they saw the original email.
- Set up a tracking tool to see who/when emails have been received and opened.

The HR representative's goal is to establish clear expectations around how and when employees will be receiving HR-related messages so that employees are familiar with the process. The HR representative should also take on the responsibility of ensuring employees are familiar with the means through which they receive information and requests and understand when it's important to respond.

LEVEL TWO: ACTION, QUESTIONS, GOALS: INTERNAL CUSTOMERS

ACTION

Employees are confused about how to set up their new benefits accounts, so they do not enroll in the program.

QUESTIONS

- Did the benefits team adequately explain how the program will work for each employee? What format did they use (i.e., printed material, video, etc.)?
- Did they host a webinar or session or provide another opportunity to answer employee questions about how to enroll in the program?
- Did they explain the steps of how to enroll in the program in a simple and easily digestible email?
- Did the benefits team provide enough information and resources about the new plan (i.e., plan overview, link to provider website, the phone number to speak to a plan representative, etc.)?

GOALS

- Send out links to program information and resources in a well-organized email and ask employees to share specific questions directly.
- Set clear and direct calls to action and deadlines in every email.
- When an action is required after a specific email, always add "Action Required" to the beginning of the subject line.
- Host a live webinar with employees to review the program and answer questions, then share a recording of that webinar with the whole staff via email.

For Level Two, the benefits team's goal is to ensure all potential gaps in understanding are filled through refined communication practices. They will develop clear, easy-to-understand messaging and leverage several communication tools to accommodate individuals who take in information differently so all team members will clearly understand what's being offered to them and the steps to enroll.

LEVEL THREE: ACTION, QUESTIONS, GOALS: INTERNAL CUSTOMERS

ACTION
Employees are interested in participating in a new goal-setting program and begin the task but are distracted by their daily duties and don't complete it.

QUESTIONS
- Have employees been given time for a goals working session during which they can focus on goal-setting without distraction?
- Does the company display any follow-through on goal-setting?
- Has the leadership team shared the importance of setting goals and that the time spent will be respected by the rest of the company?
- Has the leadership team met with other department heads to prioritize the importance of goal-setting?
- Has leadership worked with each employee to block time on their calendars for goal-setting?

- Has the leadership team ensured they are not distracting employees during that time and asking more from them?

GOALS
- Set up a goals session to teach employees the value of goal-setting and how to set their goals.
- Find and share statistics of the impact goal-setting can have on personal/professional development and on company/department achievements.
- Build accountability and focused time with leadership by scheduling one-on-one sessions to discuss where each employee is on their path to setting their goals.
- Meet with other department heads to ensure they understand that their employees will need focused time between project deadlines for goal-setting.

For Level Three, the leadership team's goal is to find ways to clear the time and headspace for their employees to feel they can complete the task. They are working to limit the number of distractions to prevent their employees getting stuck at Level Three and not completing the goal-setting process. That means minimizing potentially redundant meetings and developing deeper understandings of what employees perceive as roadblocks to productivity in their days.

LEVEL FOUR: ACTION, QUESTIONS, GOALS: INTERNAL CUSTOMERS

ACTION
When asked, employees take an HR survey that requires less than two minutes to complete.

QUESTIONS
- How is the company showing the employees that they are listening to the survey responses?
- Is the company replying to each employee thanking them for their time?
- How did the company develop the questions? Does the intention of the survey align with the company's Seventh Level Statement?

GOALS
- Share the survey responses with employees to showcase what is important to the organization and how the company is taking action on their results.
- Contact each employee who participated using their preferred communication method to thank them for their time.
- Create a postsurvey plan of action and share it with employees to let them know how their answers will be used and that their time is valued.

At Level Four, the company's goal is to acknowledge employees who have completed the desired action and thank them for it.

Showing appreciation for those who do what's requested is a simple way to maintain employee engagement and opens the door for future, higher-level engagement as well.

LEVEL FIVE: ACTION, QUESTIONS, GOALS: INTERNAL CUSTOMERS

ACTION
A company rolls out a monetary incentive program for employees to reach their goals.

QUESTIONS
- Is this the right incentive to capture the employees' interest?
- Does this incentive align with their brand values and beliefs (i.e., their Seventh Level Statement)?
- Do employees see the value beyond the incentive?
- How will this incentive aide in continued quality of productivity?

GOALS
- Survey employees to ask what they value most (i.e., paid time off, coffee, lunch, classes, books).
- Get the leadership, employees, and other stakeholders behind the larger company mission that this program works toward achieving.
- Establish clear guidelines around how goals should be aligned with workloads in order to balance the employee's

desire to achieve and their desire to win the incentive.
- Find and implement additional options for incentivizing employees that are value-based rather than financial.

At this level, the company should carefully consider potential incentives before selecting one to offer to employees in return for them meeting their individual goals. It's important to be sure that the value of the incentive is commensurate with the value of what it will produce for the company. Level Four requests can increase interaction, but maintaining or growing that connection generally requires Level Five engagement in the form of this sort of incentive. For optimum impact, the incentive should align with the brand and the brand's employees' personal values and beliefs.

LEVEL SIX: ACTION, QUESTIONS, GOALS: INTERNAL CUSTOMERS

ACTION
Employees feel a connection to the company's core values and start to adapt them to their personal lives.

QUESTIONS
- What are the company's core values?
- How are they sharing their values? Internally and externally?
- Are their values relatable?
- Are they showing pride in their values (i.e., posting about

them online, painting on the wall, printing cards for employees)?

- Do they "live" their own values in everything they do?

GOALS

- Establish a list of core values that align with your company's Seventh Level Statement.
- Provide an opportunity for employees to participate in the development of those values.
- Share those core values with all employees.
- Plan exercises to explain each core value and provide examples of how each value relates to the work the company does.
- Build a platform for employees to share examples and stories of how they and their team embody the core values.

At this level, the leadership team's goal is to inspire their workforce to feel connected to and live by the core values espoused by the organization. (It goes without saying, but this will only happen if your company's values are worth embodying—and gets back to your Seventh Level Statement being of the utmost importance!) Once employees feel deeply aligned with your company, it is important to regularly nurture that inspiration and foster even deeper engagement by continuing to "live" and strive for those core values in the actions the company takes. Then take opportunities to commend exemplary employees who live those values in order to continue to inspire others to do the same.

SEVENTH LEVEL: ACTION, QUESTIONS, GOALS: INTERNAL CUSTOMERS

ACTION

An employee becomes a brand ambassador, not only telling others about the amazing products/services they offer but going as far as to refer the company to their friends seeking employment or the services the company provides.

QUESTIONS

- How is the company aligning their employees' Seventh Level Statements with their own to build the company culture collaboratively?
- What are they offering these employees beyond financial incentives, in long-term emotional benefits, so they remain loyal to the company?
- How are they making it easy for these employees to share about the company and what it stands for?

GOALS

- Launch an employee appreciation program in which they highlight employees who are brand ambassadors.
- Provide employee brand ambassadors a platform on which to share their passion and ideas.
- Increase employee goal-setting and company follow-through—build pride in achieving goals and company growth.
- Identify a way to guide potential employees in finding their own Seventh Level Statements during the interview process.

- Only sign contracts with people/companies that align with the company's Seventh Level Statement.

At the Seventh Level, a company should be prioritizing making its top-performing and most bought-in employees feel appreciated for their hard work and dedication to the organization's goals and values. In doing so, the company continues to prove itself to be a great place to work and also maintains a top-notch relationship with its employees most likely to go above and beyond—and recruit more Seventh Level talent via referrals. One way to accomplish this is to create an ambassador program that enables Level Seven employees to travel to events or recruiting sessions on behalf of the company, which provides them with a platform to speak to their experiences, shows they're appreciated and respected, and gives them a fun opportunity to represent and engage with the company in new ways.

GUIDING QUESTIONS

1. How do I know who I should talk to? Who am I talking to? Who will resonate with my Seventh Level message?
    A. Goal: Identify who your customer is and how you talk to them.
        i. Who are you talking to? Who is your customer? Who is your audience?
        ii. How old are they?

iii. What do they read?

iv. What social media platforms do they use?

v. How do they like to be talked to?

vi. Where do they like to be talked to?

vii. What tools do they use to communicate?

2. How do I communicate my Seventh Level message? How do I get my message across?

A. Goal: Ensure you are using the right language that is easy to understand once you know who you are talking to.

i. What are the jargon words you should avoid?

ii. What is the simplest way to describe your offerings so an eight-year-old can understand it?

iii. How can you ensure that your audience understands what you are talking about?

3. How do I limit distractions so that my customer can follow the path I create for them?

A. Goal: Make sure you are not creating more distractions for your customer.

i. What is the user journey for your customer?

ii. What distractions limit your customer from doing what you ask of them?

iii. Are you creating distractions for your customer?

4. How do I communicate this Seventh Level message through instruction/requests?
   A. Goal: Ask your customer to do something that will build your relationship with them.
      i. What are you asking your customer to do?
      ii. Why are you asking for it?
      iii. Once you get a response from your customer, how do you build momentum from it to build a more meaningful relationship with your customer?

5. How do I ensure that I create an opportunity to build off of my customer's self-interest?
   A. Goal: Identify interests that are valuable to your customer and ensure that those interests align with your Seventh Level message.
      i. What is my customer passionate about?
      ii. What does my customer like?
      iii. What types of incentives will attract my customer?
      iv. How can I utilize these incentives as a mechanism to build a more meaningful relationship with my customer?

6. How do I express my Seventh Level message to inspire others to transform their own lives/set goals?
   A. Goal: Share my story so that others are inspired to share their stories of transformation.

      i.   What are my values?

     ii.   What are my goals?

    iii. How have these goals impacted my life?

    iv. How can I share the stories of those goals from others?

7. How do I personally align with my customer's personal values and beliefs?

   A. Goal: Create opportunities to stand for what I believe in and ask others to join me.

      i.   What does my customer believe in?

     ii.   What does my customer stand for?

    iii. What does my customer connect with?

ACKNOWLEDGMENTS

There is no way I could have done this without the support of the entire CatalystCreativ "family." This is not just a book but a labor of love, as it has been something I have kept close to my heart for the past ten years but didn't really know how to bring it to life. Every person at CatalystCreativ has gone above and beyond to help turn a dusty old thesis paper into a full brand and book. Aley, thank you for caring so deeply about this work that you have put your heart and soul into making this become a reality. Paul, thank you for reorganizing my thoughts better than I could. Mike, thank you for the dedication you have put in from day one at CatalystCreativ and the work you have done into building not only one brand but two brands at the same time. Abbie, thank you for keeping everything in order and going above and beyond to essentially help operate two businesses at the same time and help keep my head on straight. And last but certainly not least, Robert, thank you for being with me from the beginning, building out something we believe in together that has manifested itself in this book.

Now to my biological family. Dad, thanks for pushing me to think differently about my potential and always telling me I can be anything I wanted to be. Mom, thank you for playing such a large role in and remembering every tiny detail of my life and recounting the stories to me with so much pride and love; it helped me throughout this process to realize what makes me, me. Melissa, you work harder than anyone I know on what you love, and you inspire me to do the same. I am so proud of all that you have accomplished and the work you do for the world. Grandma Pearl, thank you for being someone I can always turn to for advice and talk to about anything. You have helped me grow into the person I am today.

To my husband, Jonathan, there aren't really enough words to thank you for all that you do as a partner. You have always supported me on every single dream and have done everything in your power to help me accomplish them. Thank you for always reminding me to have the confidence to go after what I believe in. I love you so much.

To Chaz, my best friend, and dog, you will never read this or understand this, but I will give you an extra treat for always being at my side while writing this book, whether

I was on the couch, in the house, in the office, at my desk, or traveling on planes. Thanks for trying not to bark as much as you usually do so I could actually focus on getting this done.

To Josh, thanks for being an informal advisor to me since I was eight years old. You have always been the friend that has helped remind me that I can handle whatever is in front of me.

To CatalystCreativ clients, partners, Catalyst and Creativ Week attendees, friends, supporters, advocates, and vendors, and everyone who has helped us get to where we are today, THANK YOU for believing in us, for supporting us, for caring about us, and for giving us your time and the chance to support you.

To Tony, thank you for taking a chance on me, seeing something in me before I think I even saw it, sharing your insights, lessons, futuristic thinking, network, and ability to see things that not many people see with me. I am so grateful to have met you, I can't imagine what life would be like if I didn't.

To all of you who have been there for me through everything, who have given me advice, guidance, love, support in the lowest and highest of times, thank you. You know who you are.

ABOUT THE AUTHOR

HOW LIVING MY SEVENTH LEVEL
LED ME TO MEET TONY HSIEH

After producing the Summit Series on the cruise ship, I was asked to produce a similar event in Lake Tahoe, California. People paid a high-ticket entrance fee to attend the Summit Series and hear advice from successful entrepreneurs. Tony Hsieh was one of the speakers.

In one of the after-hours events, Tony, in his typically spontaneous way, invited everyone who was in the group to Las Vegas. I took his invitation seriously. I thought I'd been singled out, and so, after flying across the country, when my car pulled up in front of his apartment complex and I spotted him,

I went to hug him hello, and he backed away. I was mortified that I'd flown across the country and now questioned whether he'd truly invited me. Only later did I discover that he invited everyone to check out his $350 million revitalization initiative.

A friend and I were in a car going to Zappos with a third person. I asked the third person a lot of questions, trying to figure out his Seventh Level—a hobby of mine. He mentioned that he lived in New York and Hawaii, and that he believed in having few possessions and being happy. I said he should watch my favorite TED Talk, entitled "Less Stuff, More Happiness."

He was in the front seat and turned around to say, "That's me. That's my TED Talk. I have a beard now, so you probably didn't recognize me."

I think what happened is when Tony heard the story, he probably thought it was hysterical. He texted me shortly after I put my foot in my mouth and asked if I wanted to have drinks with him, along with the guy I told to watch his own TED Talk and some other friends. I walked into DCR, a dark bar in downtown Vegas, and sat at the table with Tony—who blatantly said in front of everyone, "I don't really remember you,"—Graham Hill, whom I'd told to watch his own TED Talk, and my friend. Another gentleman joined us.

Tony asked me what I wanted to do with my life. I said, "I really believe in the art of using events in marketing for better and to make a difference in the world."

The man standing next to me said, "My name's Chip. I know a little about that." I said, "Are you Chip Conley?"

Chip Conley is a thought leader in the hospitality industry who has written multiple best-selling books and been on the TED stage more than once. I'd met a lot of business pundits at the Summit Series, but these incredible people were completely out of context for me in downtown Vegas.

Tony started laughing again because I'd just put my foot in my mouth for the second time in twenty-four hours. Truth is, I was simply being myself, asking questions to create community and connection. In my opinion, Tony's Seventh Level is connecting with everyone's truest self. Tony wants to know who you are and doesn't want to be pitched. He wants to see you for you—and he certainly saw the true me that day. A series of conversations began over drinks that evening in downtown Vegas.

Tony invited me to meet for coffee the next day. I stayed up all night reading his book to know who he really was. I realized he wouldn't care about any of the pitching stuff. He was a weirdo just like me. Then the next day, I repeated that what I really wanted to do with my life was to use events and marketing for better and make a difference in the world.

He said, "Do it in Vegas."

I categorically said, "No." I lived in New York City and had no intention of trading the Big Apple for Las Vegas.

Months went by, and Tony and I kept in touch. When he was in New York, he arranged for me to meet more of his friends. His right hand, Mimi, called after several months to suggest I start a marketing agency and take on downtown Vegas as my first client. I didn't know how to begin to write a business plan. I knew how to create successful events and marketing campaigns. I could build a brand and engage an audience, but a business plan was not my jam. I started crafting my ideas with Sharpie pens in composition notebooks. Six months after meeting Tony in Las Vegas, we met at a barbecue and I walked him through my colorful "business plan" notebook. Tony and I shared a lot of the same philosophies. Sitting on the grass, our Seventh Level Statements collided: mine to inspire and educate with his to create coalitions, community, and connectivity in Downtown Vegas.

With my best friend, Robert Fowler, who wanted to be able to use his understanding of experiences to beautify the world, and with Tony Hsieh, who provided a small amount of seed funding, we founded CatalystCreativ, a creative marketing firm.

During her career as an educator, Amanda realized that any platform can be a classroom with the right perspective. She learned to listen deeply to the young minds around her, and applied her teacher's appetite for active, informative engagement to develop the award-winning brand engagement firm, CatalystCreativ.

As Co-Founder and CEO of CatalystCreativ, Amanda has counseled global, national, and local organizations in planning for and achieving their branding goals. Through projects with Coca Cola, the Raiders, Google, WeWork, NPR, the Nature Conservancy, and the New York City Ballet, Amanda was featured as a Forbes 30 Under 30 honoree in Marketing and Advertising. She tells her clients, "Brands are the best teachers in the world; they just need the right curriculum."

And she sees that curriculum as the chance to truly connect with her clients' customers and inspire them to act. Amanda guides brands to do good for the world without having to sacrifice their bottom line. To do this, Amanda utilizes her well-tested proprietary method for quantifying and scaling engagement for employees and customers. Known as the Seventh Level Engagement Framework, this technique springs from Amanda's expertise marketing to millennials, Gen Z, and those she has coined as "the millennial minded."

She's spoken at SXSW, TED, Summit Series, and INBOUND about how the Seventh Level Engagement Framework is the future of meaningful, personal connections.

Amanda's groundbreaking thought leadership has been covered by *Inc. Magazine, Forbes, Fast Company, Wall Street Journal*, and *Time Magazine*. In her spare time, she is an angel investor and proud advisor to several nonprofits and companies.

She lives in New York City with her husband, where she continues daily to lead thinking on the intersection of marketing and education and develops pathways to capitalize on their overlap, all while doting on her darling cockapoo, Chaz.

You can find her at:

- The-SeventhLevel.com
- CatalystCreativ.com
- AmandaSlavin.com
- LinkedIn.com/in/amslavin/

CPSIA information can be obtained
at www.ICGtesting.com
Printed in the USA
FSHW010626070220